ANASAZI
LEGENDS

ANASAZI LEGENDS

Songs of the Wind Dancer

Lou Cuevas

Library of Congress Cataloging-in-Publication Data

Cuevas, Lou 1946
  Anasazi legends : songs of the wind dancer/Lou Cuevas.
  p.cm.
  ISBN 0-87961-256-8 (pbk)
  1. Apache Indians—Folklore. 2. Apache mythology. 3.
Legends—New Mexico.

E99.A6 C84 2000
398.2'089'972—dc21

99-087981

ISBN 0-87961-256-8

Cover painting and illustrations by Joel T. Ramirez

Naturegraph Publishers has been publishing books on
natural history, Native Americans, and outdoor subjects
since 1946. Please write for our free catalog.

Naturegraph Publishers, Inc.
3543 Indian Creek Road
Happy Camp, CA 96039
(530) 493-5353

Books for a better world

*This book is dedicated to my grandmother,
Francisca Bernal de Che, Tribal Curandera. For
her, I recall these stories which she patiently
explained were the legacy of our heritage and in
particular her parents. Her spirit is the gentle
companion which accompanied the boyhood
memory of my grandfather.*

*My grandmother taught me this maxim:
"Few realize that the life one is living
is the life others dream of."*

Contents

Introduction

During the summer of my tenth year of life I accompanied a dozen boys from the reservation selected by a clan elder to visit the spirit mountain. All of us were anxious to learn his secrets. For who better to teach them than Jhuna Ta-ta Che, the tribal medicine man, my grandfather?

As we hiked up into the dense forest, Grandfather invited reverence for the many spirits who lived there and whom he said were our kin. He spoke of Mana-lok-a, the mountain cat, whose children had been stolen from her centuries ago. He recounted pridefully the story of J-J-Wa, the timber wolf who roamed the woods in search of vengeance for the banishment he suffered. He recalled Wae-new-a, the agile warrior whose descendants became the big horn sheep. Yet the most inspiring story he related was the tale of To-Mo-Ka, the man with hands of iron.

During our stay on the mountain, often around a warm campfire, Grandfather chanted stories of wandering warrior spirits, emphasizing the importance of trust and courage. In great detail he reminded us of our history, our heritage, and the spirit bond we had with all the forest creatures. He stated they were the ancient race (Anasazi) from which we Ndee (later known as the Apache) descended.

One night, I and the other boys sat quietly around the fire as Grandfather enthralled us with his magical stories. The hour grew late and the glowing red embers splashed light warmly across his wind scarred face causing it to shimmer with mystic iridescence. He was speaking reverently of the ancient ones who inhabited the woods, when our camp unexpectedly exploded into disarray. An adult grizzly bear searching for food calmly wandered into our camp. His great shaggy form glowed in the dim light of the fire's embers, which he skirted with muffled snorting.

Terrified, the boys sitting around the fire scattered in all directions. I was no different. I shot up in terror. In my haste, I ran directly into the fork of the log, snaring my ankle. The harder I struggled, the tighter it held me.

During the confusion, when everyone else sought safety, grandfather remained seated stoically on his rock. From my position on the ground, I screamed in fear for myself, and then for his seeming lack of concern. My panic doubled when the bear discovered that one of the boys had not escaped. Me!

The odor of burned honey, dried fish, and rotting meat enveloped my face when the bear's black nose sniffed at me. Sobbing, I closed my eyes and waited for death. It was then that Grandfather arose slowly leaning against his walking staff.

As the bear contemplated where to began his meal, Grandfather's deep, resonant voice erupted aloud with a spiritual song of an ancient time. His reassuring voice stirred my memory with the legend of To-Mo-Ka and his heroic stand against invaders. In the battle to safeguard his people, To-Mo-Ka fought unafraid despite certain death. Grandfather's chant now reminded the bear of his former life among our people, his valiant deed and how he was honored as a spirit guardian of the woods.

Grandfather reminded the visitor of his pledge not to harm the children of the tribe. However, if combat is what he sought, he would accept the challenge. The moment Grandfather began chanting, the bear ceased sniffing me and approached him. The old man continued his song even as the grizzly approached. Coming within a few feet, he stopped, snorted and sniffed. Then from my trembling position on the ground I beheld an occurrence I will never forget.

Shaking his shaggy head from side to side, the bear growled at the old man who stood unafraid with his hand held upwards. Amazingly, the bear rose to a similar stance and held up his paw. Grandfather stopped singing briefly and spoke gently to the bear. Finally, he thanked the ancient one for remembering his promise and wished him well on his journey.[1]

From behind the trees, their branches, and from my position on the ground, we all remained astonished as the bear lowered himself. Following one last snort, he disappeared into the woods. For the longest time we remained frozen exactly where we were, while Grandfather slowly returned to his rock.

The story of what we had experienced echoed a thousand times back at our village. From that time on, the children stood in reverential awe of the medicine man, something the adults already practiced. In my case, I developed a deep abiding respect for my grandfather and everything he taught me.

---

1   Among the many spiritual rigors an Apache medicine man must endure before becoming a tribal shaman is one in which he shares a spiritual union with creatures of the sky, desert, or the mountains. This event is usually consecrated on his sabbatical fast on the spirit mountain.

The Legend of Shi-a-lee

The ancient Ndee, who once roamed the boundless Southwest, claimed the open territories as their birthright. Despite their many travels, the different settings, or the longevity of stay in any one place, their way of life changed little from generation to generation. In both their sedentary and their nomadic life, the average life span ensured that children lived and mirrored the culture and customs of their ancestors. To explain the reason for this chosen destiny, if it was called into question, it was sometimes necessary to recite the legend of Shi-a-lee.

The story was said to originate with a small band of Ndee who for several seasons had decided to live near what today is known as the Big Snake Mountain. In the time of the ancient Ndee, the area was called the Yellow River [Tu titsog ntuii]. The thickly forested brown and green land remained flat, dotted with mounds of round earth, and crowned with the spacious Rocky Mountains in the western distance. Though its moist black soil yielded an array of colorful prairie flowers, its main feature remained the river.

The Yellow River was a gentle, writhing body of water with slow-moving currents. Its headwaters remained secret for centuries. It cut a wide, winding path through the forested hills as far as the horizon. This was the area where the Ndee had chosen to establish their village.

The Ndee were a simple people whose peaceful lifestyle would radically change to a warlike tradition as more barbaric tribes migrated down the continent from the north during later centuries. But in the ancient time, they were content to live day to day with only modest desires. The men hunted and were quite skilled at providing a varied menu for their families. Their quarries consisted of plains and valley animals, among them the antelope, the deer, the moose, the bear, several types of game birds, and even an occasional mountain sheep.

The women, whose task it was to prepare these hunting trophies as wholesome dishes, added their own assortment of fresh produce. Items such as small-eared maize, squash, field onions, a variety of berries, and chilies helped to spice up many an occasion. The women were quite adept at cooking. Their creative talents also included basket-weaving and the making and painting of pottery. In addition was their never-ending task of mending and sewing and, of course, caring for the children.

If the daily tasks proved boring, the women were often found wandering alone in the hills. If questioned, they could claim they were searching for herbs, roots, or berries. In actuality they were quietly reflecting on their lives. This was not an uncommon habit. Many a woman wondered whether, if she had done things differently, life could have been otherwise.

One such woman, young and dark-haired, was named Shi-a-lee. Her youthful, oval face encased a set of dark almond-shaped eyes which accentuated her smooth, sculptured face. Her high-gloss cheeks were gently curved and often revealed a radiant smile which she wore without effort. Many a brave was mesmerized by her striking beauty, and, in some cases, warriors made open advances to her parents stating they were seriously interested in the daughter.

But all these love-struck young men remained outside Shi-a-lee's conscious thoughts. She knew that her parents would choose the right husband for her when the time came. After all, it was the custom of her people that if any man was interested in her, he would have to prove himself worthy in her father's judgment. This entailed much. Not only was the suitor customarily expected to be an adequate hunter and trapper, he was also counted on to protect his chosen one from all harm including that from the natural elements.

In return for his physical abilities, the young girl, when wedded to her intended, was expected to combine all of her acquired skills with his. Together the two young people (usually married in their teens) were expected to be happy or at the very least content with their mates.

If, in the course of time, the paired lovers discovered their choice was not the best decision they had made, if they were unhappy or disillusioned with their spouse, there were limited provisions in the customs of the Ndee which would permit a couple to divorce. If they were granted one, it was usually at the inordinate expense of double or triple the gifts the suitor had offered in the first place. In addition, the husband was usually humiliated and disgraced to the point of complete dishonor. Thus, divorces were nearly unheard of.

However, these thoughts were far from Shi-a-lee's mind. At that moment the striking Indian maid was on her way to the river bank to draw some water. She passed other young girls who were in the process of doing the same thing. Nearing the bank of the reed- and rush-encrusted river, the youngster was teased by her friends. They giggled and remarked to her that her older sister had already married by age fifteen. Shi-a-lee replied that she was not in the least bit worried. Her beauty would win her a loving and lasting marriage, something her tormentors would lack.

After the playful encounter, her best friend, Kemma, who had joined her at the river, complimented Shi-a-lee on holding her temper. However, she added quite truthfully that, although she envied Shi-a-lee and her beauty, the price her father was demanding might prevent her from marrying at all.

"I am not worried about it," defended Shi-a-lee. "My father's wisdom has never brought me unhappiness. I do not believe he would prevent me from marrying or give me over to someone who in his opinion is unworthy."

"But suppose he marries you off to some old goat," her friend persisted. "It's possible, you know. Look at what happened to Little Bird or Snow Flower. They were married off to much older men. It could happen to you. After all, you are not unaware that one of your suitors is Bending Tree. And he is three times your age."

"If my father chooses Bending Tree as my husband," Shi-a-lee concluded, taking a jar of water from the river, "then I will honor my father's decision without complaint."

"You poor girl," remarked her best friend. "I would fight that decision up through the Council of Women. After all, we may not have a voice, but our mothers as a group have one. They would speak for me."

"My mother has already discussed it with me," explained Shi-a-lee. "She also would never bestow sadness on me. As I said, my father understands what is best. I trust his judgment."

"I wish my father were that wise," sighed her friend, leaving Shi-a-lee at the edge of the river filling the second of two jars.

Although she believed what she had told her friend Kemma, Shi-a-lee nevertheless considered what her life would be like married to a much older man. As she contemplated such a possibility, an eerie feeling came over her. She felt the powerful sensation that she was being watched. She could not shake it from her mind. Briefly she put the second jar down beside her and looked about.

The river's flow was constant and not the least bit noisy. Occasionally fish would pop up from its glass-like surface. The green woods behind her were equally silent. The scene was picturesque and idyllic. Birds were on the wing and clouds added majesty to the sky. Everything appeared quite pleasant. Still she could not shake the feeling that she was being observed. It was a warm spring day, and yet she felt chilly. Goose bumps began dotting her tan skin.

The sounds of silence were everywhere, and despite her intense search she saw no one. Leveling the amount of water in the two small jars she carried, Shi-a-lee lifted the pair and turned from the river's edge to return home. Abruptly, she dropped both jars to the ground as she was confronted with a brilliant apparition of smoke-filled light.

The daylight was bathing the surrounding forests, and Shi-a-lee was hard-pressed to look directly into the wondrous cloud of smoke. It was immense and lay across her path like an uncoiling snake. Deep from within the cloud's center an enormous figure began to appear. Shi-a-lee was struck dumb and felt herself nearly faint as the image became distinct. It was a man.

The figure was tall and well-proportioned, and the child was immediately struck by the fact that he was nearly seventy years old. Despite the aged appearance he was dressed in the finest warrior's garb Shi-a-lee had ever seen. He held a large, well-seasoned spear in his left hand and a great war club in his right. His clothing was new and made of leather and bear skin. His face wore the tell-tale lines of many a personal combat, yet the girl felt an immediate attraction to his windswept features.

"You are my woman!" boomed a masculine voice. "You will always be mine."

Shi-a-lee's eyes widened to their limits. She fainted. It was several minutes later when she felt the coolness of water droplets touch her face. They were being sprinkled from her best friend's hand.

"Are you all right?" asked Kemma, noticeably concerned.

"Did you see him?" questioned Shi-a-lee as she came to her senses. She then began searching the nearby trees and river edge.

"See who?" repeated her friend staring incredulously.

"The man, the warrior, the..." Shi-a-lee caught the blank gaze of her best friend and saw the look of worry. "I saw a man."

"I saw no one here," replied Kemma, wiping the forehead of Shi-a-lee. "When I realized you had not returned from the river, I came back to see what was keeping you. I saw you on the ground and ran to your side. I saw no man about."

"I tell you Kemma," began Shi-a-lee, rising with her two jars still laden with water. "I saw something I have never seen before. I was frightened at first, then..." Again Shi-a-lee sensed her friend was doubting her sanity. "Forget it. Perhaps I bumped my head into a tree branch or something."

"That happened to me once before," remarked Kemma happily. "I can remember a time when..."

The two youngsters walked off towards the camp with Kemma explaining her misadventures and Shi-a-lee trying to puzzle out her strange encounter. What had she seen, she asked herself. It was difficult to concentrate with her friend talking, but she was sure something had taken place. Or had it?

That night, after the family had eaten, Shi-a-lee took her mother aside and related her story in great detail. Her mother listened most attentively and her gaze never left her daughter's dark, glossy eyes. When her daughter finished, she immediately called her husband and both sat awed by the story which Shi-a-lee repeated without effort or alteration.

"What can it mean?" asked the wife of her husband with a worried expression. "Is it possible?"

"There is only one man who can explain such apparitions," advised the husband. "Our daughter must visit the lodge of the medicine chief. Such encounters are rare and she will need his guiding hand to lead her through the forest of dreams."

Although the parents of Shi-a-lee believed their daughter, they had a great deal of doubt about the event's significance. To determine its meaning, their daughter had to present the gifts of water and soil, along with a personal gift to the medicine chief. Shi-a-lee took a newly made ram skin coat to the old man, and, as custom dictated, placed it outside the medicine man's lodge.

Shi-a-lee took up a position just outside the tepee of the mysterious medicine man and sat down. It was the custom that any member of the tribe who wished to see the medicine chief presented him with a gift at his door, and then, holding the further gifts of water and soil in his or her hands, sat and waited. It was unusual that one had to wait long for the medicine man to appear, but there were occasions when the mysterious maker of magic allowed visitors to wait long periods of time, to test their desire and commitment.

In the case of Shi-a-lee, the wait was short. A heavy, rotund old woman came to the door and took up the coat. She then signaled for the young visitor to enter. Shi-a-lee had never had reason to visit the medicine chief before. She had heard all sorts of mysterious tales of his power and magic. As she entered, she became engrossed in observing the many drawings and colorful symbols displayed on the inner walls. There were also skeletal heads of dead animals hanging from above.

As Shi-a-lee continued to stare, the large, rotund woman who was wife of the medicine chief, indicated where the young girl should sit, then, almost magically, she disappeared.

"You are the daughter of Two Bears," began the medicine man in an eerie voice. "Your mother is Red Elk Woman. You have an older sister. Your younger brother died five snows ago. You are unwed."

Shi-a-lee was impressed with the old man's mental powers. She wondered silently where he had acquired such facts. Was it his memory or that of his wife which he now called upon? She stared silently at him with growing apprehension, afraid to turn away. She said nothing as she studied his ancient, deeply ingrained features. His name was Black Cloud, and Shi-a-lee guessed him to be approximately eighty years old. His weather-beaten face could easily have been made into a ceremonial mask. It was painted heavily with white clay and streaked with black lightning bolts. Blood red dots appeared by his ears and descended to his feathered necklace.

The old man sat cross-legged across from the sitting girl; his grotesque features were further heightened by the red glow from the circular fire. In his thin arms, which lay across his lap, were two objects. One was a painted gourd with animal shapes on it. It hissed like a rattlesnake when the old man lifted it. The second was a feather. Shi-a-lee recognized it as belonging to an eagle.

"The knowledge of your family is written in the fire," he said fixing his glazed gray eyes on the frightened girl. Shi-a-lee wasn't sure whether he was able to read her thoughts. She had come to question her vision at the river's edge. Did he know that too?

"You had a visitor at the river," the wise one stated abruptly.

Shi-a-lee was now positive the medicine man was able to read her thoughts. She drew back, sprinkling a few grains of dirt which she still held in her hands in front of herself, followed by several droplets of water. These were earth signs and her mother had advised her to use them against displaying fears while in the company of the shaman.

"You may speak your fears little one," reassured the old man. "I will give you what knowledge you are able to comprehend. But understand that what you are told is valuable only if you accept what is revealed by the fire spirit."

"I am told you can interpret my vision," began Shi-a-lee with noticeable hesitation in her voice. "I was confronted with a figure in a cloud. From the inside of the cloud, a bright light came forth and turned into a man. But he was an old man, someone whom I have never seen before, yet..."

"Yet?" echoed the voice of the old man.

"Yet I thought for a moment I knew him," she said thinking back on her encounter.

"Did he say anything?" questioned the old one.

"He said I was his woman," replied Shi-a-lee recalling the voice, "that I have always belonged to him."

"Listen closely, my child," counseled the wise one. "You have had a single vision. I assure you now, he will return again and again."

"I am afraid of him," confessed Shi-a-lee. "I am sure he means to have his way. I will belong to him unless I can fight him somehow. You must tell me how."

"What you must do," advised the medicine man, "is nothing. You must live as though he does not. Your eyes have seen tomorrow. Your heart will feel yesterday. You will see that he is only as real as your fear. In the end, you will become who you were. Do not be afraid. When the light of day becomes the morning, so too will your vision."

Completely muddled by these words, and with her head spinning, Shi-a-lee made her way home. Despite her best efforts, she could not make the words any clearer to her parents than they were to herself. Explanation became a harder task when her friends questioned her about the advice. Regardless of who heard it, none could explain the prediction. Shi-a-lee was forced to live with the puzzle.

It was not long after her encounter at the river's edge that she was told to come to her father's tepee. Upon arriving, she saw that her mother and father were sitting outside the tent. Her father was sitting on the ground and before him stood a handsome young man who appeared to be a brave of some twenty years of age. Shi-a-lee recognized him as the son of the warrior, Dark Moon. Many times she had seen him, and, like other girls her age, she had come to whisper his name.

"I am called Little Wolf," stated the lad as he stood proud and erect before the tepee of Two Bears. "I am the eldest son of Dark Moon, my father, and White Bird, my mother. I stand before you now to ask that my gifts be accepted for the hand of your daughter Shi-a-lee. It is my desire that she should be my wife."

"What besides your many gifts do you offer that will promise happiness for my daughter?" questioned Two Bears.

"I am a full-fledged hunter and warrior of our people," responded Little Wolf. "I will try to be what you would ask of a son. I will bring no disgrace upon you. My life is my bond before you, and my friends whom I have brought as witnesses to my words are here to speak for me."

Thereafter a dozen men came forward and spoke proudly of Little Wolf's courage and skill. Several others, who were related to him, offered additional gifts. His two uncles produced offerings of food and a promise of a great banquet for the whole tribe. Two Bears was impressed with the gifts and the testimonials given on behalf of Little Wolf. Concluding the boy was worthy, he called Shi-a-lee forward and announced to the gathered crowd that Little Wolf had permission to marry his daughter, and he announced the joining day.

The wedding day of Shi-a-lee was fixed for the next appearance of the new moon. Until that time Little Wolf was permitted to woo his intended in any fashion he desired. It began with long walks and many secluded visits. In the beginning, the young girl was cordial enough, but did not return his favors. She knew who Little Wolf was, but she remained aloof.

Shi-a-lee had known of Little Wolf. He was easily recognized in the Ndee camp. He had indeed won the admiration of many, including other eligible maids. Yet it was Shi-a-lee whom he preferred, and to this end he labored. In the beginning, she just listened to his words of praise for her beauty. She was warmed by his long and well-rehearsed sentiments of love. He told of occasions where he had seen her walking to the river, climbing up a hillside, or merely grinding corn in front of her tepee. He confessed that he longed to be with her and promised he would try to bring her happiness.

As time passed, Shi-a-lee allowed herself to be won by the love-struck Little Wolf. Yet in her heart there lingered the memory and words of the visitor by the river. Indeed, a few weeks after her encounter with the man in the vision, she beheld him again.

When the vision returned, Shi-a-lee was better prepared. This time the image was more pronounced, and his appearance more vivid. Regardless of the risk, the young maid was determined to gain more details to offer the medicine man.

"You have always been mine!" stated the glowing man.

"Who are you?" asked Shi-a-lee, kneeling before the figure in the cloud. "What do you want of me?"

"I love you now and always," replied the voice, seemingly unaware of her question.

Shi-a-lee strained to see details, but the vision faded and she fell unconscious. Much later, when she was discovered, she claimed to have slipped on a rock. The explanation was accepted and few questioned her. Shi-a-lee hoped that she would one day come to understand the visitor. For now, she concentrated on becoming the wife of Little Wolf. Perhaps that would cause the vision to go away.

Not long afterward, Shi-a-lee was married, and, true to his word, Little Wolf proved to be an honorable husband. The ceremony was magnificent, and the festival which followed was memorable, but the most important element which Shi-a-lee would always remember was the love Little Wolf offered her. His friends and many of her relatives presented the couple with many fine gifts. In terms of custom, tradition, and the necessities of life, the newlyweds were very fortunate.

The vision Shi-a-lee had encountered seemed to vanish with her wedding day. For many months there were no more incidents. Life for her took on normalcy and even monotony. The only times she did not consider tiresome were when her husband returned from his many excursions. Then, and during the brief days he remained at home, she felt full of joy, and life seemed whole and complete.

Little Wolf had a unique ability to rekindle his love for Shi-a-lee every time he saw her. Her love for him grew in proportion to his embraces, which numbered beyond her memory. The two were deeply in love and those who knew them soon came to envy them. In time, when the years seemed all too brief, Shi-a-lee learned she was with child. The news created fear, anxiety, and much apprehension. She became unsure of herself. Fortunately, her mother brought her comfort, and, through her friend Kemma, she learned how fortunate she was.

The news of Shi-a-lee's pregnancy created a gamut of feelings among the people of her tribe. Her parents were proud and elated. Some relatives and friends were filled with praises. Others were envious and showed little interest.

The person most obviously elated by the news of a child was Little Wolf. Upon hearing the news, his joy exploded in a triumphant shout which was heard across the entire Ndee camp. His friends grinned and smiled at him. His father and mother praised the couple. Had not the majority of his people known of his joyful reason, they would have considered him mentally unbalanced.

Little Wolf's happiness was boundless. His friends saw that he never seemed to tire of describing his future plans for his children. His grandparents and those of Shi-a-lee were equally enthusiastic about their granddaughter's pregnancy. In all, between the adulation, congratulations, and gifts, the two youthful parents were hard-pressed to find any sadness in the upcoming event.

The novelty of becoming a mother never seemed to wear off for Shi-a-lee. Each day and night brought with it a new sensation or additional conversation with her friend Kemma. The two were nearly inseparable now. Their friendship doubled when the news surfaced that Kemma herself would soon wed. Shi-a-lee was convinced that her life was riding the high wind of happiness.

The happiness that Shi-a-lee and Little Wolf experienced multiplied dramatically with the birth of their first son.

In the fullness of time, the child became the focus of their lives. However, with him also came new responsibilities and additional worries as the couple joined the rest of the tribe in preparing for the changing days. Season followed season and with each change of the year their ability to care for each other and their son and growing family was tested and retested.

Several years later, when Shi-a-lee's family was the mainstay of her existence, the vision returned. It happened as she was walking across the immense prairie on a beautiful spring day. The day was clear, and the sky canopied the earth like a great blue bowl. Great fluffy clouds mantled the mountains in the distance. Shi-a-lee could see the horizon in every direction. Inwardly, she was content with her life.

As she walked, a peculiar sensation came over her. She felt as if she was being watched. She had experienced this feeling before. Summoning her inner resolve, she turned and before her appeared the mystical apparition. The cloud was gigantic. Its brilliance outshone the light of the spring day.

With her mouth gaping open, Shi-a-lee was unable to speak. The colossal male figure of an aged Ndee warrior stepped from the cloud. It was the same individual who had appeared to her on previous occasions. This time, however, while the vision spoke to her, Shi-a-lee studied his face intently. She saw that the man's eyes were familiar. Despite the fact that the figure was nearly seventy, his face seemed to belong to someone whom she should recognize. She concentrated hard, but the image disappeared. Shi-a-lee was sure he was no longer a threat. A feeling of self-confidence swept over her.

When Shi-a-lee walked back toward the camp, she was met by her lifetime friend Kemma. As her dear friend neared, Shi-a-lee was suddenly and keenly aware that her friend had matured over the years into a full-blown woman. How odd, she thought, Kemma was a year or two younger than she. Her friend appeared winded, as if she had been running. Reaching Shi-a-lee, Kemma related the news that Little Wolf had returned from a lengthy scouting expedition. Several of the men in the party had been attacked and seriously injured, and he was one of them.

The fact that Ndee territory had been invaded was not uncommon. Throughout the generations of their history, the Ndee had become increasingly aware that more and more wandering clans were migrating across their land. What was of grave concern was that incidents in which Little Wolf and other braves were injured were increasing. It became obvious that being a defensive warrior was not sufficient. Emphasis on becoming more ruthless was needed to combat the savageness of the aggressors.

Shi-a-lee spent a great deal of time tending to her husband's wounds. Over the following years, this task became routine. Moreover, the physical ability of the Ndee to withstand great pain, hardship, and deprivation, as well as to fight tenaciously against overwhelming odds or any enemy became legendary. Shi-a-lee's pride and that of the tribe's womenfolk swelled. But there were consequences of this accumulating fame. The men became increasingly hostile, solemn, reserved, and emotionally distant from their women. A gap was being created between what the Ndee once were and what they were of necessity becoming.

Women like Shi-a-lee experienced their husband's emotional change firsthand. Her emotions became tempered as well. Throughout her life she had nurtured her son and several other children to adulthood without complaint. All were given a similar chance at happiness, the same that she had received. But she was never quite the same woman after the day she learned of her first son's death, or the day after she learned of her daughter's kidnaping. At first she blamed Little Wolf, then the invaders, and eventually herself. In the end, however, she accepted the series of recurring tragedies with understanding.

Nearly fifty years had passed since Shi-a-lee became the bride of Little Wolf. Having raised five children and buried three of them, she was quite aware of life's precious brevity. During those years, she had experienced the pain of her parents' death. She had seen her long list of relatives and friends dwindle during the many wars that had devastated the peace of the tribe.

Shi-a-lee was a different woman now. She was stiff, yet dignified like a great oak tree. Her heart still beat with love for her husband, but she had seen him harden with every new conflict. She became accustomed to his silent, melancholy moods. She had seen her own tribe's land shrink with the influx of other tribes. There was much sorrow in her memory.

Among the most unhappy memories that Shi-a-lee carried in her heart was that of Kemma, her best friend. She recalled how on an otherwise humdrum winter day Kemma and she had gone searching for firewood. She remembered well how her friend was joking when, unexpectedly, she broke through the river's thin, icy covering, and, despite Shi-a-lee's valiant efforts, had drowned. Shi-a-lee mourned Kemma's passing for nearly a year. Life was never the same without her happy, playful friend. Shi-a-lee had experienced much and with the onset of old age had become a source of knowledge and wisdom to younger women who had problems.

Then one day in the sixty-fifth year of her life, in the middle of what would later be known as winter's last snow storm, Shi-a-lee took ill. For days she lingered in pain and suffered greatly. With a fluctuating high temperature, her pain-racked body pitched and heaved with hot and cold bouts of conflicting symptoms. She hallucinated that she was dead. She saw her friend Kemma and her buried relatives. She visited with dead spirits. Those who attended her were convinced she would die.

The storm was severe, and for four days it raged unabated. However, with the fifth day it subsided, allowing warm weather to renew the hearts and minds of the Ndee as well as their land. When the storm passed, so did Shi-a-lee's sickness. The days that followed were hot enough that those who attended the recovering old woman suggested that she lie in the hot sun outside the tepee. Shi-a-lee welcomed the fresh air. From where she lay she could see the children playing, the men repairing their weapons and hunting equipment, and the younger women grinding corn and gossiping about family matters.

From her vantage point, Shi-a-lee could study the whole camp. Fires were burning everywhere, and the smell of food blanketed the drifting atmosphere. The day was beautiful, with just a touch of chill in the air. Her people were out and going about their business as usual, and she was beginning to feel better. Unexpectedly, a young girl about fifteen years of age came and sat down next to her. She asked Shi-a-lee for permission to grind her corn and ask her some questions at the same time. Shi-a-lee consented eagerly.

"Have you had a good life, Grandmother?" asked the girl.

"I have had a very good life," replied Shi-a-lee, propping herself up a bit.

"Has anything special ever happened to you?"

Before Shi-a-lee could answer the girl's question she noticed a cooking fire near her tepee which was creating great spirals of smoke. The morning sun was rising and gave the ivory columns such a brilliance few could view them directly. Yet despite their harsh brightness, Shi-a-lee stared into one of the circles and saw a man appearing from within it.

Shi-a-lee smiled when she recognized the tall figure approaching her. He was an old but fully experienced warrior, wearing a new set of ceremonial clothes. His right hand carried a well-worn spear, and his left held a war club. The old man's face was haggard, but had such a proud countenance that everyone gave its wearer due respect. The man was now the chief of the tribe.

His name was Little Wolf. As he neared his life-time companion, Shi-a-lee asked him if he still loved her. Smiling broadly, he responded proudly, "I have always loved you."

Little Wolf appeared to glow as he walked towards Shi-a-lee. With the sun at his back and the clouds of smoke wreathed about him, he gave the impression he was part of a vision. Little Wolf was unable to see himself silhouetted against the morning sun, and therefore was not affected by it. Unaware of his backdrop, he stepped through the coiling rings of smoke and knelt down next to his wife, Shi-a-lee. Gently stroking his wife's forehead, he smiled down at her. He was truly glad she had lived through her illness.

"You have always belonged to me," he stated proudly. "You will always belong to me. From the time when I first stood before your father's house, and until our spirits are joined in the sky above us, and our lives become the memories of our children, you and I are joined by our love. Never forget that, my wife." Reaffirming his statement of love to her, Little Wolf rose and entered the tepee.

Shi-a-lee said nothing as the meaning of the mysterious vision she had first experienced as a child suddenly became clear to her. The vision she had witnessed during her younger years was nothing more than a vision of her own future. One nagging question puzzled her at the moment. Had she seen her future, or had she only revisited her past in the brief moments of a morning apparition? She stared into the fading smoke, trying to reason it out.

"Did you Grandmother?" repeated her granddaughter, unaware of the aging matron's inner thoughts. "Did you ever have anything special happen to you?"

The child's soft voice helped to break Shi-a-lee's concentration. She looked into her granddaughter's beautiful, almond-shaped eyes and said, "No, my child. Nothing special. Every experience I have ever had was ordained by the Giver of Life. Many may wish to daydream of what it would have been like to be someone else. This serves only to question the worth of a given life. All lives are worthy of being lived. If you wish happiness in yours, live as though you have seen your future, and it is the one you have."

The Legend of the Faithful Brother

Apaches have always maintained that spirit power can and does influence their lives. This invisible extension of the celestial creator, whom they refer to as the Giver of Life, controls their destiny. In order for the Apaches to tap into this powerful spirit source, they must learn its origins. The primary allegiance they owe to him begins with remembering their ancestors. It is the ancestors who secure and maintain power for them.

Power in Apache mythology manifests itself in the natural world in different forms. It is the circle of life. It is both the living and the dead, the dark and the light. It is the serious and the comical. It is nature, the world, and everything that makes the natural world grow.

In the desert, for instance, the hostile land itself drains the essence of man. Apaches know that to exist there, they must obtain power. Thus, Apaches believe the universal force that gave them life constantly demands it back. The Power must be satisfied they are worthy. Realizing this, they fervently seek new power.

Apaches believe that power exists in all things. The stronger beings are, the more power they have. By this equation, humans possess great power. The descendants of the ancient Ndee would use this belief in future wartime confrontations.

In the Before Time, the strongest power to be found was in the spirit world, where live the Ancients. Apache chants recall a time when the world included these spirit forefathers. Although they are long since gone, modern

Apaches believe their spirits have become a living segment of the world we inhabit. Now the most influential of powers exists within the sacred myths.

The musical chants of the storyteller remind the listener that all living things are important and necessary. Although it resides there, power cannot be taken from nature, only secured from other men. But it can also be won by being "one" with the land. Nature, my grandfather said, is the circle of life, and within her memory live the first people. In the Before Time, they were called the Ndee. This is one of their myths.

The tribe was celebrating the birth of many children in the Year of the Two Rains. Among those born was a child given to a couple who already had a ten-year-old son. Still, the couple was pleased he was born healthy and free of physical problems. From the moment of his birth he became the delight of his parents. He was a beautiful child and often sought the attention of all with his unique cry.

When the baby desired attention or merely a face above his cradle, he would cry in an unusual way, different from the typical cries of other infants. Parents, friends, and neighbors alike smiled at the feeble efforts of the baby. Try as he might, the best he could manage was a noise which imitated a wolf puppy or a playful chipmunk. His voice was sweet and perky, and the cry mostly resembled a sharp yelp.

Because of the child's particular way of crying, the father of the child named him Little Desert Voice *Ni'sigani tichane*. But this was modified by the boy's friends as he grew. They called him Little Voice. Everyone grew to like him, with one exception, his older brother.

The couple's older child was a strong, healthy lad of ten who was already on the verge of acquiring a place next to his father on the hunting path. His father, a seasoned warrior named Shaking Rock, was proud of his older son and was so impressed with his strong loud voice when he was born that he named him Walking Thunder *Ed'di.* The family was proud of the manner in which the lad carried himself. Many predicted that Walking Thunder would one day rule the plains.

For the first ten years of his life, Walking Thunder received the attention of his father. He woke early to go on long hunting trips with him. He joined him in nearly every trapping expedition and spent a great deal of time learning from him how to live in harmony with the land. During this period of time, he acquired a working knowledge of his people's craft, their way of life, and how he fit in as a productive member of the tribe.

Walking Thunder was taught everything his father knew about the lore of the animals and the hidden secrets of the land. Shaking Rock taught him well. If ever Walking Thunder wished to pick up the shield of the warrior, he would need everything his father had taught him to achieve a measure of success.

In addition, Walking Thunder listened intently to the social lessons given him by his father. These were the responsibilities of manhood. Walking Thunder learned everything from courtesy and respect for his elders to how to carry himself with dignity before other tribes. Nothing was left to chance. If there was any area that Shaking Rock failed to delve into, it might have been tolerance for a younger brother.

From the moment his brother came into his life, Walking Thunder failed to understand why he had come. In the beginning all he noticed was his father and mother's labors multiplied. Furthermore, they seemed hard-pressed to make the house stores yield enough food and the daylight hours yield enough time for the four of them. With the addition of his younger brother, Walking Thunder received less of his parents' attention. All the desire he had to prove himself to his father was soon replaced with annoyance for his brother.

As the years passed and Walking Thunder became an adult, his life became routine, his tasks merely obligatory. The excitement he had felt while hunting and trapping seemed to wane. He continued to enjoy a modest success, but he expressed little desire for more. There were many in the tribe who still admired Walking Thunder and reasoned that one day soon he would take a bride. Before that occurred, however, he would have to amass gifts worthy of one.

In the same period of time in which Walking Thunder grew to manhood, Little Desert Voice had become a likable boy of ten. His exuberance was contagious, and his circle of friends yielded quite a following. His father and mother were pleased that everyone liked him and knew he was well-accepted in the camp. Still they worried that his being an annoyance to his older brother had become a problem for Walking Thunder.

In the years before a young man reaches adulthood, there are several stages which are critical to his earning respect and honor. In the case of Walking Thunder, those segments were laced with an assortment of humorous stories which he hoped would eventually be forgotten. The stories made very little difference to the opinion of anyone who knew the truth of them, but they mattered very much to Walking Thunder. He had to live with them.

It all began when Walking Thunder was close to fifteen and nearly a man by tribal standards. The day had come when he had to prove himself to his father and several older members of the tribe and all the instructions given him on woodland lore would be put to the test. Walking Thunder was given the task of entering the woods alone, without weapon or tool, to track, stalk, and kill his first hunting prize. The only requirement was that it be large enough to warrant pride in the accomplishment.

Little Desert Voice was so proud of his older brother that he asked if he could go along. Fortunately, Little Desert Voice asked this question of his childhood friends instead of his parents or elders. Adults would have been angry that anyone would interfere with a test of manhood. However, his friends all giggled and said that it would be fun to go along but had to be done without Walking Thunder's knowledge.

The test began when Walking Thunder surrendered his weapons and crafting tools to his father. Thereafter, with an acknowledgment by his elders, he set off from the camp alone. Walking Thunder was completely unaware that Little Desert Voice had already informed his parents that he would be camping in the mountains for several days with a friend's family. Since this was partially true, his parents suspected nothing.

Three days into his test, Walking Thunder found the beginnings of his basic tools. With rocks, fire, and skill, he fashioned one series of weapons each more advanced than the other. Eventually he crafted the rudiments of a knife, spear, and a bow. These were crude examples of his craft, but were sufficiently deadly to complete his assignment.

In the meantime, Little Desert Voice, anxious to see his brother's progress, hurried to join his two friends, who, with finer tracking skills than Little Desert Voice, managed to find Walking Thunder's trail and observe him. In the end they were impressed by how talented Walking Thunder had become. Three days into Walking Thunder's labor they saw that he already had a bow and several arrows.

With the skills taught him by his father, Walking Thunder found and tracked a large elk. Then, with a precision acquired by patience and effort, he closed in for the kill. He was unaware that just a hundred yards away Little Desert Voice and his friends were spying on him.

The younger boys did not realize that the trail, recently used by Walking Thunder, was also habitually prowled by a mean-spirited grizzly bear. The curious boys lay close to an overhanging ledge which overlooked the valley floor. Down below their shrub-covered position, they could see Walking Thunder making silent progress towards the unsuspecting elk. Walking Thunder dodged stealthily in and out of tall hedges.

Little Desert Voice and his two friends were in awe of Walking Thunder's ability to move so silently. With Walking Thunder only twenty yards away from his quarry, Little Desert Voice held his breath so as not to make the slightest sound. The air came hard and his nose doubled its volume. Then, unexpectedly, Little Desert Voice caught the strong, sickening, overpowering odor of burned honey.

Walking Thunder took an arrow and placed it onto the draw string of his bow. Then, with the elk moving casually across the valley floor and into his sight, he prepared to shoot. The thin leathery line cut into his fingers as he pulled it back and held it. The elk, which up to now had been lazily grazing suddenly caught the honey scent and froze in place.

The overpowering honey aroma detected by Little Desert Voice was suddenly smelled by his friends. Without realizing their movements could alert and scare off Walking Thunder's prize, the young boys sat up and looked over their shoulders. There directly behind them was a giant grizzly with a bulbous black nose, sniffing them.

What took place next would later be recited by the three boys when they were brought before their elders for discipline. The grizzly's face, close enough to touch, was inching closer to Little Voice's best friend, who screamed in terror. The shrill scream set in motion a series of events.

The grizzly bear reached out to grab the nearest boy who in turn leaned back, causing him and his friend to drop over the edge of the cliff. Little Desert Voice reached to steady his two friends, but their combined weight pulled him backwards with them. The screaming trio now plunged over the overhang and directly onto an outcropping of thick foliage.

Meanwhile, the elk had caught the scent of the bear, then heard the boy scream and vanished, causing Walking Thunder to miss his target. A few seconds later, Walking Thunder heard the cries of his brother and his friends as they sought escape from the grizzly, who was trying to find a way down the side of the cliff.

Walking Thunder raced to help his brother. He quickly decided to cross the knee-deep river and to climb the earthen embankment on the far side. The soft dirt, rocks, and high wall of shrubbery angled up some thirty feet. Without hesitation he began scaling it.

The thorn-studded briars clawed at him like an angry cat, but Walking Thunder seemed not to notice them. His mind was focused on the descending bear and the screaming boys, who were running out of room for retreat. With his best estimate of the height of the ridge ledge and the possibility the bear might reach his brother first, Walking Thunder doubled his efforts.

In the meantime, the two friends of Little Voice closed their eyes and hugged one another for protection. Keeping his own eyes open, Little Voice realized that he and his friends would have no better chance against the roaring bear than against the thirty-foot drop to the boulders below. Then, out of the corner of his tear-filled eye, he saw Walking Thunder scrambling up towards him. Instantly his heart leapt with joy, pride, and respect. The danger of the approaching bear dwindled, and his own courage held.

The enormous grizzly bear, which towered over eight feet tall and equaled the weight of five grown men, was enraged and frustrated at his inability to reach the terrified boys. They were just below the thick ledge and slightly away from the overhang. The bear managed to stretch within inches of the nearest boy. Straining further, the bear nearly slipped off the sandy edge altogether.

Instinct drove him to strain harder across the jutting overhang, nearly snatching the nearest child. Tossing his head from side to side in anger at having a meal just beyond his reach, the bear pounded the ground and roared repeatedly. His murderous frustration echoed like thunder in a ceremonial drum. Determined to succeed, he again stretched out, leaned over, and growled at the stricken boys, who were convinced the bear would reach them.

Only a few scant yards separated the bear and the crying boys when Walking Thunder saw the Grizzly peering over the cliff. The bear was unconcerned with Walking Thunder's efforts, and he continued to edge his massive bulk over the cliff edge, straining in earnest. In this attempt, he momentarily snagged the nearest boy, who screamed in agony as a deep gash opened in his arm. Seeing the bear nearly tumble over when he came close to securing his prize, Walking Thunder got an idea.

Making his way up and across the clawing wall of brambles, Walking Thunder selected a spot just below his brother and waited for the outstretched arm of the bear. While adjusting his own precarious position, he removed his deerskin shirt. Because of the razor-like thorns, his face, chest, arms, and hands were oozing blood. Cleaning his wounds with the shirt, he offered it upward to the extended claws. The ravenous bear caught the scent of fresh blood and became doubly enraged.

The bear again stood up and pawed savagely at the ground. Then, pausing to growl again, the bear lay down to try to reach his intended victims. Instead, he caught the bloody shirt offered him by the waving arm of Walking Thunder. The bear caught the shirt, but only briefly. Urged on by instinct, more and more of the bear's gigantic body leaned over the cliff, and, with a powerful lunge, he finally caught the elusive shirt.

Anticipating that the bear would have to lean forward for the blood-scented shirt, Walking Thunder allowed him to snare it. Once the bear took hold, its prodigious strength surprised Walking Thunder with a sudden upward lurch. However, as Walking Thunder had also expected, the hulking beast's position became vulnerable. With his body as a counterweight, Walking Thunder pulled downward with every fiber of his being, and the unsteady creature fell headlong over the cliff.

The moment the bear crashed onto the massive boulders below there was great relief in the eyes, hearts, and minds of the three boys. While they remained huddled together, trembling, Walking Thunder climbed up past their position and secured himself at the top. Once there, he braided several vines together, and, then, with some coaxing from Walking Thunder and cooperation on each boy's part, he pulled them up one at a time.

When news and details of the event reached the village council, there were mixed emotions. Many elders and parents praised Walking Thunder and chided Little Desert Voice and his friends. The elders were not sure whether the combined act of heroism and killing the grizzly bear warranted completion of the task given to Walking Thunder.

In the end it was decided that Walking Thunder had acted wisely and courageously. It was the many gaping wounds he sustained in his climb to save the boys that won over the council. Still, some doubt remained with those who suggested that Walking Thunder had been extremely fortunate. They said a hand-to-hand encounter with a grizzly bear could have left him dead, and that his act of courage could simply be attributed to circumstance.

Though he was given a measure of respect by the tribal elders, Walking Thunder could not force all the doubting whispers to go away. Once the parental punishments had been completed by the three boys, Walking Thunder took his brother aside and added his voice to those who had already admonished him for being foolish.

"I am trying to set the standard of manhood for myself," explained Walking Thunder angrily. "You cause me great embarrassment. Why don't you leave me alone?"

"I am sorry my brother," sniffed Little Desert Voice through a stream of tears. "I only wanted to see how you would succeed. I did not mean to spoil your chances."

"People in our tribe think I am not a man," Walking Thunder added. "I will prove them wrong if you will just stay away from me."

"But I am your brother!" defended Little Desert Voice. "I must repay you for saving my life."

"Do that by staying away from me!" finished Walking Thunder, moving away. "I am trying to become a man and you are making me wish I never had a younger brother. If you want to help, stay away!"

With his brother's angry words echoing in his mind, Little Desert Voice spent the next few years seeking to repay his older brother for saving his life. There were many attempts, but each failed miserably. There seemed no way to help Walking Thunder. Each try only succeeded in provoking Walking Thunder further.

In the same year that Walking Thunder celebrated his twentieth birthday, Little Desert Voice reached his tenth. There were celebrations and special events for both boys, but the celebrations of his older brother were forbidden to Little Desert Voice. This was the year Walking Thunder could prove himself to his prospective bride.

Among the many events that Walking Thunder was privileged to attend was his first sweat lodge. The religious house was filled with many of the tribe's dignitaries and some were there to ask the younger men what they knew about the spirit powers. The elders expected the younger men to breathe in the hot vapors of the black lodge and to recite from memory their spirit lineage.

When it came time for Walking Thunder to recite, he was prepared. He had worked long and hard to memorize his family's lineage. However, when Walking Thunder was only halfway through his recitation, a serious fire broke out in the village, and everyone scrambled out of the sweat lodge to extinguish it.

The sweat lodge is a holy place and the Ndee use it to cleanse themselves of spiritual impurities. Once inside, there is nothing more important than to concentrate on what is happening to one's spirit. Nothing is supposed to disturb the participants inside the lodge. If conversation is engaged, then only the speaker and the listener are allowed to communicate. Otherwise, only chanting and prayers are allowed.

This event tarnished the ceremony of Walking Thunder. He was well into his recitation when the fire alarm was given. The men in attendance and those who were servicing the sweat lodge scrambled to alert those inside that someone had set fire to a nearby tepee, and it was in danger of destroying the sweat lodge.

In the inquiry which followed, it was discovered that several boys were tending a fire which created the heated rocks for the sweat lodge. The boy in charge was Little Desert Voice. When he learned his brother had been invited into the holy ceremony, he volunteered to help heat the rocks. After the rocks are heated to their peak temperature, they are taken in a large basket into the sweat lodge.

Little Desert Voice tried to ensure that the stones he and his friends provided were the hottest ever given. However, one of them was so hot it caused the wicker basket to burst into flames. When the boys saw the fire spread rapidly onto a nearby tepee, some ran off to give the alarm while Little Desert Voice attempted to put it out himself.

Because Little Desert Voice was unsuccessful at putting out the fire, the flames leapt into the sweat lodge. By the time the fire was extinguished, it had ruined the ceremony. Walking Thunder had to wait several months to repeat his testimony, but eventually he succeeded.

Although very few people blamed the boys, one of those who had the most to say to Little Desert Voice was Walking Thunder. He tried to remain calm when he spoke, but Little Desert Voice saw that Walking Thunder was holding back an enormous amount of frustration and anger.

"You have ruined my chances to build on my reputation!" shouted Walking Thunder. "I must succeed in proving myself a man to everyone, especially the elders!"

"But you are already great in the eyes of many!" Little Desert Voice pointed out. "They speak of your courage everywhere in the village. I have heard that your name will be offered in the next elders' meeting. You will be chosen to become a warrior."

"I have heard that you are a clown!" admonished Walking Thunder. "They speak of you as the little voice behind me."

"I only want them to know that I shall always be at your side," promised Little Desert Voice. "I will be faithful to you always. You may count on me to warn you of every danger that threatens you."

"The only danger which threatens me is your presence!" Walking Thunder exclaimed, pushing his brother to the ground. "I will fight my own battles. I do not need your protection. If you want to do me a service, leave me alone! Stay away from me! Forget that you are my brother."

"That I will never do," sighed Little Desert Voice as his brother walked away from him. "I shall never abandon you in your trials. But I do promise to be a better brother."

The strained feelings between the two brothers had become noticeable to their parents. Though they tried to explain the younger boy's ambition to Walking Thunder, no argument could ease the frustration he felt. He pointed out that he was receiving snickering remarks from the giggling women and small children of the tribe.

The matter had become so difficult to deal with that Walking Thunder began avoiding his younger brother. This made Little Desert Voice feel isolated and unloved. He understood why his presence annoyed his older brother, and he yearned for the day when he could prove otherwise. There had to be a better way for the two to find common ground. Walking Thunder was advised by his parents to visit the medicine man.

Though leery of the idea that the wise one could do anything which might change the situation, Walking

Thunder arranged for a visit. According to the practices of his tribe, Walking Thunder prepared a gift and then set it before the tepee of the Shaman. He waited for two hours and then was summoned.

"You are troubled my son?" asked the medicine man, knowing full well what ailed the young warrior. "I see anger, and the shadow of your brother on your face."

"He is forever underfoot!" complained Walking Thunder, finally being allowed to vent his frustration. "I cannot go anywhere without him following. Each time I attempt to show the force I carry as a warrior, he calls out my name with that squeaking voice of his and people laugh at both of us."

"In time you will come to accept his voice and be at peace with him," promised the medicine man. "His presence is part of your destiny. You and he will share the spirit world. Nothing can change that."

"Will I ever become a warrior?" questioned Walking Thunder, desperately reaching for some solace in the old man's words. "I must know if I am to be free of the doubt I carry."

"In the future, your spirit will dominate the land," began the medicine man, his eyes closed. "All manner of warriors and hunters alike will challenge you. Your name will bring fear to those who would test your anger. Your spirit will one day be honored and men will know your name."

"Will I be rid of my brother?" asked Walking Thunder hopefully.

"He will protect you unto death," answered the shaman. "In the spirit world, he shall be known as the faithful brother. In time, you and he will live in peace."

"Never!" finished Walking Thunder. "I plan to leave him in this world when I go to the next."

Though partially satisfied with the prediction of the Medicine Man, Walking Thunder was still unwilling to accept the fact that his younger brother would one day share his fame. However, there was one comforting aspect to the prediction. There was much to secure in this life before he would journey into the next. At present he had to find a wife. In this he knew with certainty he would succeed.

The bride considered by Walking Thunder was a beautiful young maid named Dream Sparrow. Her ambition was to one day become the wife of a warrior. Thus, when Walking Thunder approached Dream Sparrow's father to offer his gifts in exchange for her hand, she had no objections. She knew of his courage with the bear and his several battles with marauding tribes. She urged her father to accept.

It was not customary for the bride to choose her husband, but it was important for many fathers to secure a measure of happiness for their daughters if possible. So it was in this case, and the wedding ceremony followed soon after. With his talent for causing trouble for his older brother, Little Desert Voice was advised to stay as far away from the ceremony as possible. This advice was given by Shaking Rock.

Realizing he might bring trouble to his older brother's wedding, Little Desert Voice decided to take a day-long trip to the nearby mountain. There, with several friends, he set up camp. They were not intending much beyond spending the day fishing along the river. However, things did not go as planned.

No sooner did Little Desert voice snare a large fish when a prowling wolf came along. Seeing the youngster and his friends wrestling with their enormous catch, the wolf decided she was a match for the group. Spotting the wolf and realizing her intentions, the boys decided to defend their prize. When the wolf approached and threatened them, the boys seized some clubs and large rocks and began throwing them at her.

The lone wolf was stunned that the boys put up such a resistance to her snarling. However, she continued to advance and warned that she was going to attack. Sensing they were going to lose the fight, Little Desert

Voice suggested that they attack first. The boys gave ear-splitting shouts, waved their clubs, and threw stones. The wolf at first hesitated and then decided she was no match for the determined group.

Buoyant from their success, the boys began a celebration of their own. They were glad to see the wolf turn tail and had no way of knowing that she was only an advance guard of a larger pack. No sooner had they packed up their prize and begun a leisurely pace back home, when the four of them heard the loud barking and growling of the wolf as it returned, this time leading the pack.

The boys had never quite gotten over their terror from the grizzly bear incident, and now their fortitude was about to be tested again. This time, the oldest boy suggested the best way to avoid being ripped to shreds was to run for their lives. Little Desert Voice and the others wasted no time arguing. They sped down the mountain with Little Voice in the lead. Fortunately for them they had not ventured too far from their camp.

In no time at all the escaping foursome crashed headlong into the merry-making of the wedding ceremony. While their parents began reprimanding the four children, one of the village sentries came speeding by and warned everyone that a pack of wolves was chasing the boys. The camp warriors instantly reacted, and soon the battle was on. The wolves had intended to set upon the helpless boys, but instead they received a hail of spears. Most of them were killed outright, but one managed to injure a member of the bride's family before it died.

When the wedding day incident was delved into, it was proven that Little Desert Voice and his friends were not responsible for the injury to the visiting guest. However, despite the excuses offered by his little brother and his friends, Walking Thunder could not help but fix blame on them for the indignities which he had suffered.

Once again, Little Desert Voice felt he had failed to keep his word not to bring shame to his older brother. Instead he had once again achieved the opposite. Not everyone felt the same way, of course. Shaking Rock and his wife and several elders tried to counsel the brothers and explained that no harm had been done. Yet, neither they nor the parents nor their friends could bridge the gulf which seemed to be dividing the brothers.

Concluding that something was missing from his life, Walking Thunder made an evaluation. He had attained manhood through the woodland trials. Because he had actively participated in several campaigns, he was accepted as a warrior. He had even been chosen for the tribal council because of his wisdom. He was a full-fledged hunter/warrior, and aside from a few who doubted his abilities, the tribe considered him to be a courageous and honorable man.

Despite his merits and achievements, there still lingered in his own mind the nagging fear that his little brother would yet destroy all he had worked for. He wondered why his brother was so intent on helping him. Had he not made it clear he could earn respect without his younger brother? How often had he explained it?

The admonition seemed wasted on the ever-present, ever-lurking Little Desert Voice. Each time Walking Thunder saw his brother's eager, round face, he made it a point to let him know he was not welcome. Yet within the disapproving tone of every chastisement, there was an inner admiration for the persistent boy. He wondered why, after all these years, had Little Desert Voice not learned to hate him?

While his older brother contemplated his life, Little Desert Voice walked alone. He was beginning to think life was too difficult. Despite everything, it seemed hopeless. Walking Thunder's dislike of him was developing into noticeable hatred. Walking Thunder had publicly humiliated him and chased him away. Little Desert Voice felt unwanted. Despite consolation from his parents, he found little to smile about. Finally, his father suggested he visit the medicine man and ask guidance from the spirits.

Following tribal custom, Little Desert Voice sat outside the medicine lodge with a worthy gift for the spirits. He expected a wait of several hours. Instead the tepee flap opened after several minutes. The wife of the shaman invited him in and left. His gift offering was accepted by the medicine man, who then asked the youngster to sit across from him.

"You have come to ask if life has meaning," stated the wise one.

"How did you know?" asked Little Desert Voice, surprised. "Can you see into my heart?"

"The spirit of a warrior is no barrier to the truth," the medicine man revealed. "Your journey is troubled by your failures; yet you persist. That is good."

"I have tried everything to show my brother I respect and honor him," confessed the boy sadly. "Yet my brother hates me! People make fun of my voice. My friends are beginning to think I will never be anything more than a clown. I am lost. Help me, Wise One. Where lies my destiny?"

"Tomorrow is destiny," voiced the medicine man, looking into the red embers of the fire that separated them. "The Giver of Life makes power. Man must fight man to keep it. Once he has power, it lives in his courage. One seeks the other and a man finds his destiny in his deeds. You are power. I tell you, one day your deeds will bring spirit power to our people. Forever, it will live in the hearts of men."

"And my brother?" probed Little Desert Voice.

"His destiny is woven into the fabric of yours."

"He saved my life, Wise One," added Little Desert Voice. "I must return a life to him. But it is hard."

"On that day, your voice will find courage and it will bring you power," concluded the medicine man, opening his eyes to the startled boy. "On that day you will be honored by your brother and our people. You will become a spirit power."

Little Desert Voice was reeling from the information given him by the medicine man. Though Little Desert Voice later repeated the words to his parents, they were not able to explain the words to him. In the end, Little Desert Voice was happy that one day he would earn the approval of his older brother. His heart felt good.

Not long after the visit of Little Desert Voice to the medicine lodge, the whole tribe was summoned to council. Once assembled, the people were informed that new tribes from the land of the Northern Plains were reported raiding neighboring villages. They were told that soon these marauders would arrive and bring war and death into the land of the Ndee.

Realizing it was only a matter of time before his people would come under attack, the old chief began making preparations. Anticipating fierce opposition, he decided to find the exact whereabouts and numbers of the enemy. To do this, he sent a scout to the entrance leading into the valley. With little hesitation, a hundred warriors volunteered for what would prove to be a hazardous undertaking. Not surprisingly one of the warriors chosen was Walking Thunder.

Not long after the enemy warriors were located, the chief and his group departed to confront them. A day later, word was received they had been ambushed and were in trouble. The council decided a second group should be sent to reinforce them. This was arranged and the chief received reinforcements just as they were being attacked. In the ensuing battle, a hundred men were killed and hundreds of the enemy were slain. Among the Ndee dead was the chief.

Although outnumbered, the Ndee stopped the relentless and punishing enemy invasion. Soon the main enemy force retreated, leaving only a handful of scattered parties to deal with. One reluctant band was particularly angry and vowed to destroy the Ndee to the last man. This did not deter the Ndee from winning several more skirmishes.

The fighting spirit of the Ndee was so great the renegade band realized they would never defeat such a formidable and extraordinary people with conventional tactics. It was decided to leave the area, but not before trying one last gamble. First they would strike directly into the heart of the Ndee camp and kill as many warriors as possible, and kidnap the women and children.

Because of a message from one of the scouting parties informing them the enemy invaders had retreated, the Ndee camp prepared to celebrate. They were unaware of the impending peril. Miles away on the field of battle Walking Thunder was made the new leader. His first order was to send men back to warn the tribe to prepare their camp before the enemy struck. Few of the replacements were aware that Walking Thunder and his original party had not slept in four days. Yet here they were, holding back the remnants of the persistent enemy.

The young boys of the Ndee tribe were used as messengers from the camp elders to the main force in the field. One of those chosen was Little Desert Voice. He and his friends felt proud to do their part in defending their people. However, despite all the messages being relayed, Little Desert Voice had only been called once.

When one exhausted runner returned to the village to warn of an impending surprise attack from the enemy, the entire village was alerted. Then, with the arrival of Walking Thunder's reinforcements, the raid was repulsed. The system of messengers worked.

Not wanting their warriors in the field to worry unduly, word was given to one of the runners to say that the enemy raid on the village had been unsuccessful. The message stated many of the enemy had been killed, and the rest had surrendered in humiliation. The message was given to a friend of Little Desert Voice.

When he realized the war was nearly over, Little Desert Voice convinced his friend to let him take the last message to his older brother. He wanted very much to congratulate him on being chosen leader. After much pleading and cajoling, the boy relented and Little Desert Voice took his place.

The marathon to the battlefield lasted five days. Though he was tired and had rested along the way, the majority of the time Little Desert Voice spent racing across the wide, lonely desert. The weather was hot, and the terrain was uneven and full of danger. Bushes, thorns, cactus, brambles, and predators often caused him delays. In addition, the blistering heat and harsh winds beat him like angry lashes. Finally, a sudden downpour nearly drowned him as he crossed an empty arroyo and almost forced him to stop.

Eventually he reached the high hills overlooking the battlefield where his brother was last reported to be. Scaling the high ground, he looked across the vast open plain and saw quite clearly where his brother's camp was located. It would take him perhaps the rest of the day to reach it. He estimated he would arrive sometime during the night.

As the sun set and Little Desert Voice ran towards his brother's camp, he suddenly realized he was being followed. Four strange-looking men in costumes he did not recognize were racing after him. Realizing he might be captured, Little Desert Voice summoned all his reserve and sped away, leaving his pursuers well behind him. It was exactly what the enemy had expected him to do.

Not turning to see if he had outdistanced those following him, Little Desert Voice raced on, hoping to reach his brother's camp soon. With his heart and lungs aching, he knew that running blindly in the desert night was risky, but he suspected that if he stopped he would be caught. In his mind's eye, he saw the camp straight ahead. However, the only thing straight ahead of him were the outstretched arms of one of the enemy warriors.

After being asked forcefully half a dozen times, the enemy concluded Little Desert Voice would not tell them what message he was carrying. It was decided torture was the only way to make him talk. However, the several methods tried produced only the exhaustion of several of the enemy. Seeing him covered in blood and tears, unconscious, and showing the signs of having been beaten senseless several times, the enemy temporarily gave up and tied him up in one of their storage tepees.

It was the loud talk of the enemy outside his confinement which awakened Little Desert Voice. From what he could gather, the enemy had discovered that the men in Walking Thunder's camp were asleep. They also learned that the sentries posted around the camp were nodding off as well. It was decided to attack at daybreak and kill the sleeping Ndee.

Though it took considerable pain and effort to release himself from his bonds, Little Desert Voice did just that. Standing up, he peered out from a slit in the tent. He suspected it would not be easy to escape. From his vantage point, he saw dozens and dozens of enemy warriors and some were leaving. He knew where they were going and that he had to get away. But how?

Knowing full well that if he cut a hole in the leathery fabric of the tent, it would alert his guards, he had to think of something else. Looking around his small enclosure, he got an idea. He found a hole in the ground directly underneath a large rug. Entering it, he dug and tunneled furiously until he came out on the outside several feet away from the tepee.

Lifting his head out of the small burrow, he was certain that if he kept very low to the ground he could escape. With meticulous care, he crawled away from his captors without making a sound. His body was racked with pain, and several of his major wounds were beginning to bleed. However, he realized if the warriors who had already left were able to reach his brother first, he and his men would all die. Despite his pain he began running.

With the fear that his brother would soon die, Little Desert Voice raced on, caring nothing for his own suffering. Scrambling across the grassy terrain with only the dimmest light, he crept silently past the sleeping sentinels and into his brother's camp.

Just before entering the camp, he spotted the approaching enemy some distance away from the sleeping encampment. They were preparing to massacre everyone with bows and arrows. Seeing that his brother's men were fast asleep, he considered what to do next. If he shouted, he would be the first one killed by the stealthily moving enemy.

Remembering how irritable his voice had become to the men of the tribe, including his brother, Little Desert Voice began softly calling the men by name. The squeaks and barks of his voice soon began to irritate and anger the exhausted warriors. One by one he called them. Those who awoke first asked him to be quiet. However, Little Desert Voice continued until all the men were awake and complaining.

Little Desert Voice could not take a chance that Walking Thunder would be caught asleep by the enemy. With a sense of urgency, he stood and loudly shouted for the men to rise and face the surrounding enemy. No sooner had he alerted the Ndee than an arrow pierced his chest. Falling, he continued to call his brother's name until he saw Walking Thunder rise.

When Walking Thunder was alerted to the approaching enemy, he instantly ordered his men to stand and repel the invaders. The whole Ndee camp awakened immediately and assaulted the enemy, who had expected to take them unaware. Instead of a quick victory the enemy was routed and soundly defeated. When they were last seen, they were either escaping across the plain or asking for quarter.

After the battle, Walking Thunder knelt over the body of his dying brother, and, for the first time, wept. He realized his brother had known full well that by standing up and shouting, he would die. Yet with selfless courage he saved not only his brother, but the men of the tribe as well. Holding his brother's bleeding, broken body, Walking Thunder praised him and promised he would remember him as a warrior.

This made Little Desert Voice proud. Smiling weakly, he looked up at his brother and swore he would return to be at his side. Shortly after his promise, and delivering the message given him by the elders, Little Desert Voice died.

With their hearts heavy from the sacrifice of Little Desert Voice, the Ndee men said little when they returned to the camp. Peace had exacted a price. Among the wailing voices at the funeral pyres which burned brightly in the evening glow were those of the parents of Walking Thunder and Little Desert Voice.

The medicine man explained to all how, in losing one life, Little Desert Voice had repaid two in return. He had given to his parents their older son's life as well as the life of his bride. He further promised that when the older brother reached old age and died, Little Desert Voice would return.

The prophecy was fulfilled in the waning years of Walking Thunder's life. When he died at the age of eighty-two, his spirit was at ease with the world. He departed, saying his little brother had returned to him as predicted by the medicine man. From that day forward they have shared the plain and are considered inseparable.

One day, while touring the desert plain, I saw a most remarkable sight. There, amassed in a great herd, were the plains buffalo in all their regal peace. Moving across the land, their numbers sounded like distant thunder. When they stopped and lay idly on the ground, I asked my grandfather who their constant barking companion was.

"That," revealed my grandfather, "is the living essence of a warrior. He is known as the Spirit Brother of the Buffalo. As promised, he is always seen at his brother's side to warn him of danger. He is a great power in the desert and plains. He is known as the Little Desert Voice." I smiled, because I recognized the Prairie Dog.

The Legend of the Magic Riddle

Since the beginning of written history, mankind has been plagued by one unrelenting and inescapable enemy: Time. It is not so much the measurement of time, but rather the uncertainty it creates that causes fear. Humans have always been consumed by the mystery of who did what first. Moreover, man is further pressed by innate fear of being forgotten. Nations who consider themselves worthy of being remembered prepare diligently for the greatest threat to their living history: Oblivion. Past Native American tribes were no different.

Within the tales of Indian mythology, there exists a myth of how a clan, living in what was then called the Ja-se-jo or the House of the Red Snake, met the challenge of time. It is remembered by their modern children through oral accounts, how they survived the battle with time. This story was related to me by my grandfather many years ago and is about a group of people who called themselves the Ndee. It was they, legend has it, who were the first children of the Giver of Life.

These children lived where they chose; sometimes it was on the plains, and on other occasions it was in the mountains. For a time, there was one clan which lived in the cliff sides of a hidden valley called the House of the Red Snake.

This term, House of the Red Snake, referred to the colorful river which wound through the vast area. Ndee history records the exact date of their arrival and the length of their stay on long knotted ropes and wide belts constructed of different colored beads. The myth remembered begins in the year of the Yellow Moon.

In the beginning the legend speaks of the peaceful Ndee and of other tribes which endlessly migrated through their land. Because the other tribes were unworthy, they faded into the darkness of oblivion. This darkness was called the lost age, primarily because many of the original races who were given the breath of life by the Great Spirit did not keep it sacred. They made war on their brothers and sisters and as punishment were lost to all future memory. The ancient Ndee firmly acknowledged the peace of the Great Spirit and promised to always live by this rule. In return, the Great Spirit wrote their name in the first pages of mankind's history, history which recorded that they would become the fathers and mothers of many races.

There are many people in this myth. The most central figure is a man called Dancing Bear. He is considered by his descendants to be the father of their clan. Beside him stands his faithful and loving wife, a woman called Little Dove. Together, they are the heart of this legend which remembers how they solved the mystery of the Magic Riddle and immortalized themselves and their people forever.

My story begins twenty years prior to the births of both Dancing Bear and Little Dove. Their parents and the rest of their tribe were then living near the Little Snake River in a secluded section of the hidden valley, called the House of the Red Snake. It was a peaceful land composed of soft brown hills, tall green grass, and was carpeted with miles and miles of colorful prairie flowers. Standing sentinel over this undisturbed beauty rose an imposing mountain covered with dark forests and sharp, overhanging sandstone cliffs. It was here that the Ndee tribe lived.

The harsh winter months which had held the land in a tight fist of snow and ice had begun to loosen their frigid grip, permitting the first streaks of sun to appear. Now, as the frosty days of winter gave way to the pine-scented spring months, the light became a welcome visitor. In the hidden valley, the billowing clouds yielded to the persistent warming trends, allowing the valley people to take great joy and pleasure in their hunting and gathering expeditions. There was much to do after the depletion of winter and the tribe was eager to begin restoring its health and vigor.

On one particularly sunny day, amid the dozens of returning, tired, and unsuspecting hunters, a complete stranger was discovered to be walking among them. Those who noticed him first were startled by his lack of fatigue and his mysterious and sudden appearance. He seemed to materialize out of thin air. When they saw him, the hunters all gathered slowly unto themselves, discussed the man, and concluded he was not one of their band.

Although the stranger who walked among them was not unlike them in physical appearance, his clothes appeared completely new, not worn in the slightest like their clothes. Though his dress was similar, they determined he was not a person whom anyone could identify. However, as it was their custom not to take action against strangers without consulting the chief, they decided that, for the moment, he should be allowed to continue among them as they entered their camp.

Since strange men were a rarity in the camp of the Ndee, when he appeared, he became the focus of the tribe's attention. The older men eyed this stranger with suspicion and caution; the younger men were curious and invitingly innocent of any danger. The women, although equally curious, gathered their wide-eyed children close as the brightly attired stranger walked further into the buzzing village. The chief, the council, and the medicine man were disturbed by the mysterious stranger, but hid their emotions behind masks of stern patience.

Unhindered, the stranger walked slowly toward the Ndee council grounds. The chief and his hunters followed at a distance, with the bulk of gawking people trailing behind them. Eventually everyone arrived, offering the chief an opportunity to study the mysterious visitor. The chief's eyes made a multitude of tiny observations. The stranger, he noted, appeared to be an old man, but retained a youthful aura. He was tall and well proportioned with limbs indicating abundant power and strength. He had a serious, rugged, and windblown face which, like his long braided hair, was black. Two deeply grooved, ashen eyes formed a taut but pleasant expression. His wardrobe was magnificent.

The old stranger who walked into the Ndee camp on that bright, beautiful day appeared indifferent to the people gathering around him as he approached a predetermined spot. Once there, he stopped. He calmly took a place and sat down. Aside from the sounds of barking dogs, crying children, and chattering women, there was little in the way of alarm. Thus when the chief saw the stranger sit near the council fire, he imitated his unexpected guest, sitting directly across from him. The braves of the tribe formed a half circle behind their chief and, although not heavily armed, presented a formidable defense.

When the tribe had quieted to hear what might be said in the inner circle of the council, the stranger spoke softly, "Are you the leader of these people?"

"Yes. I am called Little Crow," answered the chief. He was surprised that the stranger could speak his language so flawlessly.

"Then, Little Crow, I have a question for you and your people," the stranger said. "Do you wish to live in peace on this land?"

"Can it be otherwise?" the chief asked curiously. "Can you alter the fate of our children or their future?"

"One easily becomes the other," answered the stranger. "I have come to your people with a riddle. Fail to answer it and you and they will die unknown. Solve it, and you and they will inherit the world."

The tribespeople who, up until then, had remained quiet, began speaking loudly in astonishment. Yet the visitor did not react to their loud disbelief. He remained unconcerned. The chief and his council conferred, speculating that the old man might be delirious from his journey across the trackless plains. But one look into his unwavering stare and a detailed inspection of his shimmering clothes, convinced everyone that he was neither delirious nor joking.

"What is this riddle?" asked Chief Little Crow.

"Before any attempt is made to answer it," the stranger replied, glancing at the circle of people, "you must choose two from among your people. They will bear the responsibility and consequences of failure. For, you see, if you do attempt to solve the riddle, I will require a price. Since you are the leader of your people, you must choose one man and one woman. The others will die in due course. Do you accept these conditions?"

"They are harsh and unpleasant!" complained the chief. "Do we have any alternative?" With every ear listening closely to the words spoken, the stranger outlined the fate of the tribe if they refused to risk answering the riddle.

"Yes, you may decline to attempt the riddle," explained the stranger with little emotion in his voice. "Refuse and you and your people will live out their lives undisturbed and in peace until season's end. Then, all of your people, the young and the old, will perish and their memory will fade like the waning moon."

The chief and the others around the council looked hard at one another and immediately came to the same conclusion. "If we are to take you seriously," replied the chief cautiously as his people muttered to themselves, "then surely it would not be too great a task for you to give us some proof or sign that we are not being made sport of or that you are not a passing lunatic."

"One of your older women has in her care a sightless child named Dark Cloud. Is this not true?" asked the stranger.

"It is true!" shouted a frantic woman from the crowd, stepping forward through the throng. "My child has been blind since birth, five winters now!"

"Take the child to the river," ordered the visitor, staring at the chief who stared back in awe. "Reach into the stream and touch his eyes with the waters. Do it now."

Without hesitating, the woman plowed through the heavy crowd, rushed to her tepee and dove in. She exited with a small, confused boy and raced to the nearby river. With trembling hands and with the boy asking what he'd done wrong, the woman all but drowned herself and the child as they fell, kneeling, at the river's edge. With her heart pounding like a great drum, she reached into the cool waters with a cupped hand and bathed her son's eyes with them. Her heart was threatening to burst while she held her breath. Eagerly she waited, half believing and half hoping. Not wishing to have done it wrong, the anxious woman repeated the instructions, splashing her child's face again with the cool water until, at last, she drew away from the river and waited. When the boy did not open his eyes, she grew angry and carried the child back to the council circle and left him with a relative. Through anger-filled tears she walked up to the stranger and prepared to voice her rage before the tense crowd. Quite suddenly the child began to cry and ran towards his mother without aid.

From one end of the village to the other there rippled a jubilant wave of hysterical delight and joy. Happiness swelled every heart. Those who cried loudest were familiar with the sorrow of the mother and grief she had felt for her son. However, as the cheering reached a zenith, the realization came that their uncommon visitor was more than he seemed. Many were now convinced that he was a powerful spirit. Instantly, a shroud of silence fell upon the villagers whose dread and anxiety had now doubled. Anticipating further miracles, half the crowd moved closer, while the other half drew back in fear.

"When must you have our decision?" questioned the Chief. He was quite convinced that his guest was indeed serious about the wagering riddle and the tribe's fate.

The stranger's face had not changed since he had sat down. At the moment he remained calm, aware that his audience was thinking quite seriously about the future. "I shall sit here and wait for your answer," replied the stranger." I am quite prepared to wait until you are ready."

The chief, wearing a mask of strained concern, rose and made his way to the council lodge. The majority of the people openly buzzed with speculations while the council and the braves followed the chief. After a brief discussion, the council unanimously favored accepting the riddle. To do otherwise, they advised, would condemn the tribe to oblivion. The chief agreed and prayed the answer was within their collective wisdom.

"We have decided there is little choice but to accept your terms and your riddle," began the chief after returning to his magical guest. He had a young man and woman in tow. "This couple will stand for our people. What is your riddle?"

The tribe held its collective breath as the visitor stood. There had been gossip and muttering in the crowd, but it quickly and abruptly ceased when the stranger rose to study the two youngsters. They were young and quite frightened, understandably enough. Their worried expression was shadowed on the faces of all the other people.

The stranger concluded that he had the tribe's complete attention. Every eye was opened wide, every mouth gaped, and everyone seemed utterly petrified. Nevertheless, the chief noticed the absence of malice in the visitor's behavior. Indeed, the visitor did not exhibit the slightest hint of expression that he might be enjoying the frightening effect he was causing. If anything, he looked sad. After waiting a short length of time, the stranger spoke, directing his words at the surrounding crowd. "I give you this riddle that you may win a place in the future," he said. "It will determine what you will inherit. I offer one clue in the hopes it may aid you: Your mother gave you life. Your father nurtured it. All children will return to their parents. Here is your riddle.

"From water rises the land, the symbol of your fathers. The spirit of their song is the shield of your mother."

"Is this our riddle?" questioned the chief, awed by its complexity.

"It is," challenged the stranger without emotion.

"How much time do we have to respond?" questioned the chief soberly, showing deep concern.

"One day!" was the stranger's reply.

Although the wisest men of the council gave it their best consideration, they were completely baffled by the mysterious riddle. Assistance was requested from everyone in the village, but no one could unravel it. Not surprisingly, the following day the best answer the tribe could give was "a mountain!" This was the reply offered to the stranger by the chief.

"That is not the answer," responded the stranger, "and the first two lives are mine. I will come back in the cycle of one moon. You have until then to learn the answer." Finishing, the stranger took the two protesting youngsters and disappeared into the plain. Efforts to follow him proved fruitless. Those who tried were unable to discover a single track to follow. Thereafter, the tribe began to dread the dwindling of days until the next moon.

Following the eve of the new moon, the stranger again returned to the village of the Ndee. He surmised the riddle had become a great burden to their lives. Nonetheless, he politely reasserted the agreement. Reluctantly the tribe heard the riddle again.

"From the water rises the land, the symbol of your fathers. The spirit of their song, is the shield of your mother."

Again the tribe put its collective brains together and after much discussion, arrived at yet another possible answer. "It is an eagle!" offered the chief expectantly. "It skims the water, is a great symbol, and often is the source of our song."

"And where does one find the shield in the eagle?" asked the stranger.

"There was no reply from the chief or his people. Sobs broke readily enough when the answer to the riddle was discovered to be wrong. Two more of their children were about to be taken away. In desperation, several groups of men tried to attack the stranger, but unafraid and undaunted, the stranger raised a single hand and the attackers were lifted into the air and hurled to the ground. Thereafter, the tribe realized their only chance to defeat the stranger was to find the answer to his magic riddle.

Month after month, always on the new cycle, the stranger arrived to hear the different answers. It's a beaver!" tried one. "It's the tree!" attempted another. "It's the wild geese!" suggested a third. Guess as they might, not one of the next ten answers proved correct. Ten months later, the tribe became hopelessly accustomed to defeat and the loss of their young people. Each month caused the tribe's grief to deepen. Still, no one dared challenge the stranger on the fate of his victims. Too many tribespeople believed the forfeited youths were being killed and eaten.

The Ndee were a strong people, but the loss of their children was beginning to have a serious effect on their numbers. Year after lonely year, the tribe tragically dwindled from an expanding community of some two thousand to less than fifteen hundred. Their once healthy population was being systematically whittled down each month. Every cycle of the moon produced fear, and the appearance of the stranger doubled this anxiety. Still, no one could be found who could solve the riddle. Many tribesmen despaired that no hope remained.

Twenty years passed and life in the camp settled miserably around this cyclical event. By now, it was taken for granted that two people would be lost each month. Curiously, the years had not altered the stranger in any way. He had not aged, nor had his power diminished. His impressive attire was magically impervious to age and wear. So too was his mournful face.

Throughout the two decades of the stranger's visits, many children were born. Despite the worries and troubles of the parents, they believed their children alone were unassailable. In among all the newborn children, were two bright, intuitive youngsters who were full of life. Their individual families were very proud of them. The youngsters acquired the skills of life quickly and courageously, and were untouched by worry, anger, and mistrust. These children appeared empty of the fear wrought by the mysterious and recurring visitor.

To the people of the village, they were unusual children in every sense. Regardless of the tribe's sorrow, they were able to revive the happiness and contentment of the bygone years. It became a joy to see them cheerfully scampering through the campsite playing games. The boy was named by his parents according to his disposition: Dancing Bear. This was due in part to his mirthful imitations of a crazed bear cub. The girl was called Little Dove by her parents because of her small size.

The two children thoroughly enjoyed their childhood years and happily entered their adolescence. As they did, they were made aware of the awesome menace of the riddle and the risk everyone faced. Still, they remained unafraid. Indeed, as they matured, they courageously placed their names in the pottery jar from which all the pairs were chosen. They, like all others, swore to abide by the choice of the council and their chief.

Dancing Bear and Little Dove took the complex riddle seriously. Day after day, along with friends and parents, they studied the invisible meanings behind the mysterious words, never forgetting the one clue. Yet, in due course, they too became accustomed to seeing the stranger return, recite his riddle and then depart with two of their friends. They vowed to someday learn the answer. For now, all they could do was accept their own sorrow. Like their parents, they grew to hate this uneasy pact. But life had other responsibilities, and they soon assumed the roles befitting a man and a woman in their tribe. Among their chores, were the tasks and everyday duties, hunting, planting, and harvesting.

Yet, during this learning time, new and distressing events overshadowed the threat of the riddle. With the arrival of the planting season came the arrival of a migrating tribe into the land of the Ndee. As always, the appearance of strangers caused consternation. Since their unfortunate encounter with the recurring visitor, they had become distrustful of new people. Still, they held hope. Maybe the newcomers would become allies and then help to solve the magic riddle. With peaceful intentions, the Ndee visited their neighbors offering them gifts and inviting them to council. In response to this kindness, the strangers declared war on them.

It seemed unbelievable that the migrating tribe could be so savage. Repeatedly they attacked and burned the Ndee village, killing dozens of innocents and scattering the rest of the tribe in panic. The Ndee were not full-time warriors and were unaccustomed to defending themselves against such brutal people. On one occasion, a group of Ndee warriors went out to engage the enemy, but learned that they had been tricked. Upon reentering, they found their village scorched, and learned, to their grief and dismay, that their chief, the council, and two hundred of their people had been massacred. The Ndee people unable to control their sorrow, scattered in turmoil and disunity. It was then that the courage and wisdom of Dancing Bear as a leader surfaced for the first time.

Although he, too, was in favor of attacking the savages and venting his anger, his concern for the safety of the women and children came first. With this in mind, he ordered the people to first take their belongings up into the high cliffs of the nearby mountain. There he sought and found a reasonable defensive location. It was a secure campsite within the hollow confines of broad overhanging sandstone cliffs. Satisfied with the protection of the cliffs, Dancing Bear discovered several advantages to his new home. But to ensure total security, he determined everyone should take part in making dried bricks with which to construct walls, rooms, patios, and to seal up ledges, pathways, and unwanted routes leading to the interior. Though it took many days to complete, the cliff site soon took on the appearance of a well-fortified complex. It was what Dancing Bear had envisioned.

Having completed his fortress, Dancing Bear could now concentrate on the savages who had brutally displayed their treachery. Promising Little Dove and the rest of his people that the invaders would pay dearly for the deaths and destruction of his people, Dancing Bear amassed his painted, avenging braves and led them down the mountain, past the Snake River, and out into the plain.

During the following weeks, Dancing Bear sadly discovered that being a courageous warrior was not the only attribute he needed in war. In battle after battle, he learned that neither he nor his men were a match for the enemy. Though they were a determined and stalwart group, they could not compare their fighting skills with those of the marauders. As a result, the inexperienced Ndee lost on many occasions. In the end, the valiant band of braves returned wearily to the safety of their cliffs.

Once they were back home, they set about recovering from their wounds, but no sooner had they arrived, when the mystic stranger appeared among them demanding yet another couple. This time, it was Dancing Bear who met the stranger, who was impressed with the young chief. Without appearing to be intimidated, he asked the stranger to consider the condition of the dwindling tribe, pointing out that those who remained were hardly worthy to be selected. After surveying the decimated tribe, the stranger sympathetically agreed. Walking among the survivors, the visitor stopped to observe the delicate beauty of Little Dove. He concluded that Dancing Bear had chosen his wife well.

Little Dove paid little mind to the close scrutiny the stranger gave her. She continued to go about her chore of tending to the wounded and sick. After studying her intently, the stranger became enchanted with her simplicity and proposed a new agreement. If Dancing Bear and Little Dove agreed to become the next pair in the riddle contest, the stranger would consent to wait until the conflict between tribes was ended. Speaking on behalf of Little Dove, Dancing Bear refused, but Little Dove reminded him of the tribe's fate and asked him to reconsider. Unable to deny the responsibility she reminded him of, Dancing Bear reluctantly accepted. Thereafter, the stranger disappeared, granting the tribe a respite of one cycle.

Throughout their early lives, Dancing Bear and Little Dove had been drawn ever closer in their love for each other. For the young leader his responsibility to his people took public precedent over his love, yet there was nothing he would not do for her. Little Dove never expected to enjoy her lover's affections in public, but later, when they were alone, Little Dove tried to extract a promise from Dancing Bear to take her to the next battle site. Though he truly loved her, Dancing Bear refused, reminding her of the great danger, and adding that he would never forgive himself if she were harmed. Though she persisted, he remained adamant.

Weeks passed allowing Dancing Bear to believe he had sufficient stores and weapons to once again face his enemy. Bidding farewell to his people, he departed and Little Dove feared she would never see him again. In haste to avenge his losses, Dancing Bear and his men soon reached the lower woods. There, they hid their supplies and set off to find the enemy.

Though Dancing Bear's plan was carefully conceived and his fighting efforts on the plain commendable, he nevertheless was forced back to the Little River Valley where he encountered more disaster as he and his men were ambushed. Surrounded by an enemy who blocked the avenues of their escape, Dancing Bear and his meager group took a defensive position along the wide river and discovered that, en route, they had lost their supplies. The band sought protection among the enormous boulders near the river, and that night

Dancing Bear, unable to sleep, reviewed his misfortunes. He sadly admitted to himself that he had failed. Staring into the moonlit night, he prayed to the Great Spirit, while a short distance away, Little Dove slipped quietly into his camp. When he learned of her presence, Dancing Bear strongly suggested that Little Dove escape quickly, but she refused. In his weakened condition, Dancing Bear found himself too weary to argue.

The following morning three Ndee warriors went out foraging for food while Little Dove attended Dancing Bear and the wounded from the band. As Little Dove tended him and the others, Dancing Bear confessed to her his lack of hope.

The sun rose quickly and Dancing Bear's courageous group silently awaited death. Meanwhile, he and Little Dove sat idly by the river. Staring into the dark shallows they watched as a huge rock turtle swam by. As it ventured out from its watery home, it crawled up the stony embankment. Little Dove recognized it as a source of food, and captured and cooked it. While she cooked, she fashioned the shell into a kind of shield.

An hour after the band had eaten the great turtle, its shell lay on the ground. After the good meal, the spirits of the rejuvenated men began to rise. Feeling a new strength and vigor flowing through him, Dancing Bear remembered his enemies who were no doubt awaiting his surrender. Defiantly, he instructed his band to sing joyously and with abandon. Soon everyone was singing loudly and Dancing Bear, finding the turtle shell shield, banged out a cadence. His boisterous song soon attracted the attention of the surrounding but curious invaders.

The enemy chief was a huge man and, from his muscular build, anyone could easily see that he was very strong. Dancing Bear observed the giant approach and rose to greet him. The enemy stood on one side of the river while Dancing Bear and his men stood on the other. Neither man had any problem throwing his voice across the rippling stream.

"It is difficult to hear your surrender above the noise!" taunted the enemy chief. "If you'd like, we'll give you proper drums with which to sing your death chants."

"If you do not hear it," replied Dancing Bear, "it is because none is offered. As for this drum, it will serve to destroy you!"

"That is an empty boast!" countered the giant enemy chief. "And to prove it, I challenge you to single combat! Defeat me, and my warriors will allow your band to escape. But if I win, your people must become my slaves. Accept the challenge if you are so foolishly courageous."

"I accept, with one condition!" shouted Dancing Bear confidently. "If I win, your people must promise to leave our land and never return. Swear it before the Sky Father and on your people's lives."

"I willingly accept," said the tall warrior. "I swear it upon their lives."

Without exchanging further words, the great savage began to run across the shallow river with a tremendous battle axe in one hand and a leather shield in the other. Dancing Bear could see there was murderous fury in his painted face and restrained power in his arms. The sight rekindled the memory of his dead people. He seized his own war club and the shield Little Dove had fashioned from the turtle shell. Like an exploding geyser, Dancing Bear was filled with a revenging rage and sped with agility across the river to engage his mortal enemy.

He sloshed through the waters, his club in one hand and the turtle shield in the other. When the enemy chief slammed into the slightly smaller Dancing Bear, it was as though a gigantic grizzly had collided with a timber wolf. As that smaller creature would have been, Dancing Bear was hurled twenty feet through the air and slammed back into the water. However, still imitating the wolf, he instantly rebounded and snarled angrily, returning quickly to attack his immense adversary.

Dancing Bear was not raised as a savage. His skills as a warrior were practiced solely for protection. Yet deep

within his avenging heart, he discovered he was quite
capable of inflicting surprisingly large amounts of
punishment on his towering foe. During the watery
conflict, it became increasingly difficult for both men to
maintain a secure footing. Nevertheless, Dancing Bear
continued to hold his own against an obviously stronger
adversary.

As the din created by the exchanging blows became
thunderous, those on the river banks were noticeably
affected. Feeling helpless and concerned, Little Dove
flinched as the massive giant hammered down on the
shield of Dancing Bear. Her heart ached as she heard
each crashing blow. She prayed for his deliverance.

Slamming each other with their war clubs the chiefs
made a symphony of pain and suffering and the
relentless clamor continued until quite unexpectedly
Dancing Bear's club shattered, leaving only a sharp stub
the length of a knife. Discovering an additional
advantage, the giant instantly doubled his efforts. His
face reflected satisfaction and in his eye, one could see
the gleam of victory.

It was fortunate for Dancing Bear that he had selected
the turtle shell as his shield. Any lesser shield, at this
point, would have proved disastrous. However, the river
soon became an ally of the enemy. Reeling back from the
incessant blows, Dancing Bear realized that his foot had
become entangled in some underwater grass or moss.
Dancing Bear endeavored to protect himself against the
raining blows, while at the very same time, he tried to
struggle free from the tangling moss. The giant sensed
his valiant enemy was in trouble. Realizing a further
advantage, he maneuvered around his entangled victim.
Finally, the huge warrior was able to send a crashing
blow glancing off the turtle shield and into the temple of
Dancing Bear opening a large gash.

With the impact of the great stone axe, Dancing Bear
was sent careening backwards, dazed. Little Dove
fainted as she saw her lover sink below the water with
the waves enveloping him like a heavy blanket. Dancing
Bear sank quickly as if he were made of stone. Within

his bleeding head, he saw celestial objects. Envisioning himself dead, he floated off the ground, ascending rapidly. As he rose higher and higher, he could see the ground falling away from him. There was a great ringing in his head and he imagined his ears were locked inside a drum which someone was striking with a rock. Unable to control his ascent, he rose ever higher, passing over the snow-capped mountains. Eventually, he entered the blackness of space. From here he could see the continents of the earth below and this image focused clearly in his mind.

Abruptly, a drowning sensation desperately urged him awake. Flailing his arms about, he reached for the shiny blue sky above the waters and forced himself back into the reality of his more imminent danger. Surfacing with a great need for air, Dancing Bear immediately caught sight of a shadowy and gigantic form wielding an axe over him. Instinctively, he reacted by ramming the remains of his club, now a sharp stub, into the heart of the giant and pushed with all his might. In a matter of seconds, Dancing Bear saw that he had inflicted a mortal wound upon his seemingly invincible adversary. With the water streaming down his bleeding face, Dancing Bear saw the enemy drop his heavy axe and fold over dead. Dancing Bear, standing erect, reached down and lifted the dead man's head above the waters, giving a resounding shout of victory. Seeing their great champion slain in battle, the remaining savages fled in terror into the woods, and the Ndee returned to their land to rebuild their village.

The savages, however, did not keep their promise and reappeared with new intentions for war. But curiously, a strange occurrence took place on the night they were set to attack. As they stood poised to invade the Ndee camp, they all vanished. The Ndee were not even aware of their dangerous intentions and their concern remained with the stranger who once again had returned, this time to a newly constructed village.

The strange visitor entered the rebuilt camp and, as always before, sat down across from Dancing Bear who waited near the council circle. "Tell me, young chief," began the stranger with a noticeable pride. "What is the answer to this riddle:

From the water rises the land, the symbol of your fathers. The spirit of their song is the shield of your mother."

"The answer, old one," began Dancing Bear extremely confident, "the answer is a turtle. It rose from the water onto the land. It has always been a powerful symbol of our fathers. Their turtle spirits gave me courage, and I expressed it in my song. In the turtle's armor I saw the shield of my mother, the earth."

The entire Ndee tribe had gathered to hear the answer offered to the strange visitor. It was an answer which only two members of the tribe knew. Dancing Bear and Little Dove had talked at length about the events near the river and that was when Dancing Bear had found the answer to the riddle. He recalled that the stranger had given the tribe an important clue when he first came to visit, but everyone had missed the obvious: the Earth Spirit gives all life to its inhabitants and it is the Sky Father who nurtures it.

Dancing Bear was not one to forget such a memorable fight as he had fought with the giant. He had encountered death and knew upon waking that all life eventually returns to its spirit form. When that happens, there is a return to the parents, the Earth and the Sky. Thus he knew the answer to the stranger's riddle.

The stranger allowed the Ndee to hold their breath a bit longer before he smiled and acknowledged that Dancing Bear had given the right answer. Though Dancing Bear was glad, he remarked sadly that the answer, so long in arriving, had cost the lives of too many of his people.

"They never died, young man," explained the stranger. "I only took them to other parts of this land to become the parents of new tribes. You and your bride Little Dove shall enjoy the answer to this riddle as a gift for all time. I hereby grant you love, peace, and a long life. You shall have many children in the generations to come."

Standing before the assembled tribe, the stranger began to glow. Then, waving good-bye, he disappeared into the air. The Ndee instantly realized that the stranger was the Spirit of the Sky Father. Before leaving, the Sky Father had explained that the attacking savages would never return and that they had been consumed by oblivion, a fate which no longer haunted the Ndee. He promised that, from that day on, the world would belong to them. As proof he left the symbol of the turtle imprinted on the planet as his sign, a sign which today belongs to the descendants of the Ndee. If you doubt it, observe the world from a distance, from space. Study the continents imprinted upon the shell of the turtle as Dancing Bear saw it.

The Legend of the Golden Dreamer

The deep blue skies which span the vast lands of the Ndee were bequeathed to them in the beginning of their history. The heavens, the earth, the forests, and all of its creatures were their birthright.

Ndee were the forebears of the Apache nation. From them came the knowledge of the origin of all creatures. They were the keepers of this ancient knowledge.

The Ndee had a very special relationship with the "Giver of Life." (Also called the "Great Spirit.") It was believed by the Ndee that if they kept his laws, he would bless them with additional gifts which would allow them to remain strong. They learned to appreciate their spiritual kinship with him. At various times throughout the year, the Ndee would gather to celebrate and give thanks to the Giver of Life for everything he had given them.

Celebrations consisted of feasting, dancing, and chanting which spoke of proud visits, visions, or messages from the creator. Each chant related a story of how a special gift or animal had first come to be. Visions were important because it was believed that the ancient spirits could speak to the living only through these magical encounters.

In the beginning of their history, the Ndee had difficulty interpreting the meaning and strength of these encounters. In the fullness of time, they came to understand them as a link to the spirit world, often weaving each spiritual encounter into their song-like chants. One in particular, which originated in the early days of their culture, told the story of Cloud Dancer. It was a simple tale which was used by the medicine man to instruct the children on the power of spirit, dreams, and visions.

It happened a long time ago, in the twelfth year following the Black Moon. They had been good years and the Ndee had prospered in the land of their fathers. Because it was a good and sacred land, the Ndee seldom ventured far from it. For twelve turns of the snow, they had enjoyed a prosperous peace. During that same period of time, far off to the north, a powerful and violent people had begun a massive drive to the south. Their goal was to conquer and enslave all the weaker people who lay in their path.

As long as the invaders were still many months and miles away, life for the Ndee went on as usual. The beginning of summer meant it would soon be time for the long hunt. All the most experienced hunters of the tribe began restoring their spears, bows, and arrows. While they prepared for the long hunt, they also waited for the youngest men of the tribe to pass through a tribal ritual called, "the time of trial."

The time of trial signaled the maturing phase in a young man's life during which he entered manhood. The young men prepared for fifteen years studying their father's teachings for their trial at sixteen. Among the subjects taught were hunting, trapping, and hand-to-hand combat. To become a man, a boy had to prove his strength and power to earn the respect not only of his own people, but also of others he encountered.

A young man could prove his worth at any of the skills, so it wasn't necessary to become an expert at all of them. To become the very best at any of them was, however, admirable. Among the more cherished traits were courage, patience, tenacity, and endurance. These qualities would ensure a man a respected place in the ranks of the tribe. These qualities, then, were what each boy's father had instilled in his son.

For the Ndee, the whole of life was like the seasons which made up the changing year. Each stage or change had a specific time and purpose, as each season had a special meaning. A young man was like summer, daring anyone to challenge his power, intentions, or intensity. The maturing man was akin to autumn, a time which tested his ability to plan for the future. The seasoned warrior was winter, always conscious that failure here would mean death for his family. Then the spring came again, a time of renewal. For the warrior, spring was the time to expect the birth of a son. Such was the life of the Ndee who looked forward to the next season in his life.

Before the yearly summer hunt came two events. The first was the time of trial. These trials were in actuality a sequence of serious games which would not only determine the tribal future of each boy, but could also determine his spiritual destiny. From these trials, the most proficient young men were chosen to enter the ranks of the warriors of the tribe and earned the title "brave." Once a boy was granted this title, he was a full-fledged member of the advisory council to the tribal leader or chief of the Ndee.

In the second event which preceded the annual summer hunt, the tribe would celebrate this change from boyhood to manhood in a special ceremony. In the summer in which the story takes place, the medicine man speculated that most of the young men would become skilled hunters and warriors, and that one or two were destined to become something more. Among the boys who hoped to take their place in the ranks of the warriors was a lad named Cloud Dancer. His father was proud of him and had taken great care in his schooling. Ever since Cloud Dancer was old enough to understand, his father had taught him every aspect of becoming a brave.

Cloud Dancer was fully aware of the qualities required of every Ndee brave. The boy soon became adept at hunting, trapping, and fishing. He also mastered every social responsibility. Cloud Dancer's mother was extremely proud of her son's accomplishments. Sitting in front of the family tepee grinding the corn, one could see tears of joy swelling in her eyes as her son and husband returned from their woodland trips. She was amazed that her young son had perfected his skills so long before other boys the same age, and there was no denying the results: So abundant were the father and son's hunting, trapping, and fishing trophies. But she could hardly believe the stories which accompanied each prize.

With his wife listening attentively, Cloud Dancer's father related to her all he had witnessed in the several weeks he and the boy had spent in the upper mountains. Cloud Dancer was a superior boy, the husband informed her, but there was a disquieting strangeness to his abilities. He could, for instance, see animals miles away, long before they were actually encountered. Later, he could track them through the woods at night so silently, most creatures were not even aware he was there. His father considered it magical.

When Cloud Dancer stalked, his father never doubted the fate of the hunted. Even if the animal sensed its danger and tried to escape, the boy would bring it down with unerring accuracy. There was little doubt; Cloud Dancer was an extraordinary hunter with uncanny abilities. Although his success caused envy among neighbors, his parents were not disturbed. His father was proud of his son's unique skill, but what father would not be? His mother found it unsettling to learn of her son's unusual powers, for she was aware that such powers could result in misunderstanding.

With his son helping him, Cloud Dancer's father reasoned that the family would have enough provisions to last for many weeks to come. Later, as he and his wife stored their winter supplies, the father told her of the other observations he had made of their son. "He's a natural hunter," the husband proclaimed, as he proceeded to recount several astounding events which bordered on the impossible.

It had been their third week of travel into the high mountains, began the father, when Cloud Dancer waded across a wide, but shallow river. As he entered the flowing waters, the boy looked down into the clear, stone-layered river bed. From a nearby vantage point, his father could see his son searching for the large fish which occasionally swam near the surface. Abruptly, however, the boy froze in his tracks.

The father, seeing Cloud Dancer suddenly stop still, wondered what could have caused him to do so. He went to see. Meanwhile the boy continued to stare down into the mirror-like waters. There, below him in the shimmering waves, the boy could see reflected the blue sky, the passing clouds, and the occasional bird, all directly above him. But the image which should have been his own, was not. Instead it was that of some strange, wondrous being he had never seen before. Upon entering the gently flowing river, and nearing his son's position, Cloud Dancer's father could also see the glowing, golden image. He was astonished by what he saw.

The shimmering reflection in the waters which spread outwards from below his son's knees was not that of Cloud Dancer, but of an immense Indian brave evolving into an equally immense golden bird. The glittering being appeared to be shape-shifting back and forth, half man and half bird. The strange reflection of Cloud Dancer soon revealed a huge pair of golden wings, his youthful head had become the feathered cowl of a great bird with a yellow-hooked beak and two large almond-shaped eyes. The boy stood mesmerized as the shimmering image continued to change back and forth. Abruptly, the vision changed.

As both men stared wide-eyed, the golden vision began to show a much broader scene. This time it revealed the golden bird flying high above a raging river, carrying a woman in its great yellow claws. This image caused Cloud Dancer great surprise, and it snapped him awake. Cautiously, he reached down into the cold river to try and grasp it. Instantly, the image disappeared.

Sometime later, as father and son sat silently on the shore of the river cooking a fish, the boy spoke hesitantly. "What does it all mean, father?" he asked.

"It could be a blessing or a curse," his father explained, his own mind unsure of what he had witnessed. "It was like seeing a dream from a distance. As to its meaning, only one man can determine that."

"Standing Bear?"

"Standing Bear," repeated his father, nodding his head knowingly.

With the vision firmly fixed in their heads, the two hunters continued to trap and hunt in silence. Then, when their pack horses were laden, they made their way back home. Upon arriving, the boy's father advised him not to speak with anyone but the medicine man about what they had seen. More confused than frightened, the boy agreed readily enough. The father was sure that the image had a definite connection to his son. But was it a true vision or a fantastic illusion?

Unaware that his father was telling his mother of the strange and baffling vision, which had by now become a recurring dream, the boy went to the medicine man's lodge. Before the brightly painted tepee the boy placed a large cut of fresh deer meat. Then, as custom dictated, he took up a sitting position a dozen feet from the entrance and waited. The boy spent most of the morning and part of the afternoon sitting in silence.

Shortly before sunset, the flap of the medicine lodge was pushed open and an old gray-haired woman stepped out. Seeing the offering, she examined it and took it inside without saying a word. Then with the last vestiges of sunlight disappearing into night, she returned to the opening and signaled for Cloud Dancer to enter. The woman silently led him to a place near a small fire in the center of the lodge and indicated to the boy where he should sit. She then served Cloud Dancer and the old man a portion of the cooked deer meat and left quietly.

The tepee flap closed behind the old woman, and the boy looked around the dimly lit interior. It was eerie and decorated with many oddly-shaped figurines. Some of them Cloud Dancer recognized easily; others were strange and gave off ominous shadows which made the overall effect even more mysterious. As the boy took a small bite from his portion of meat, he studied the medicine chief sitting directly before him. He was a silver-haired old man with deeply carved lines indenting a rugged, aging, yet benevolent face.

The face of the medicine man was careworn, weather-beaten, and even the freshly painted lines could not disguise the fact that he was old. Yet even in age, he was someone to whom respect was given without question. No one ever allowed the medicine man to pass without acknowledging his presence, offering due respect and polite courtesy. Of all the people in the village, no one produced more uneasiness than the medicine chief. At the moment he sat quietly eating his fill of the deer meat which Cloud Dancer had offered him as a token of good will. He was dressed in his traditional garb, which consisted of a large buffalo headdress and deerskin clothes with many colorful animal pictures on it. He ate silently.

Cloud Dancer had nearly finished eating when, quite abruptly, the old man spoke in a voice which sounded like distant thunder.

"Why are you afraid of yourself, my son? Why does your spirit trouble you?"

"I only wish to understand what it means, holy one!" was Cloud Dancer's reply. He knew the old one could read his heart and mind.

"The images concern your destiny," explained Standing Bear, looking across the fire into the boy's puzzled face. "For destiny, you must be patient. Do not fear it, nor yourself."

"It troubles my heart, holy one," the boy pleaded further. "It troubles my sleep. I am not able to touch the surface of water without seeing my reflection and this golden vision. I am unsure of its meaning."

The reddish light glowing outwards from the fire illuminated the old man's face, giving it a ghostly appearance. For several minutes, the boy said nothing as the old man began to chant aloud. While he sang, he shook lightly two painted rattles. It seemed to the boy that the smoldering fire responded to the old man's song. Suddenly, a large plume of smoke rose to halo the old one as he spoke.

"The Giver of Life sends these words to you," the medicine man thundered, pointing towards the astonished boy. "Out of darkness will come the fire. Flames will bring suffering, pain, and anguish. Out of water will rise your destiny. Courage is the shield of the warrior. You are the shield of our people. Approach the new moon and be born in the waters of conflict."

The words of Standing Bear still echoed in Cloud Dancer's mind as he walked home that night. In the days which followed, he tried desperately to unravel the riddle of the old one. Yet, it proved to be impossible. To make matters worse, each time he saw his reflection in water, the image became more pronounced, and still the meaning of the image eluded him. In resignation, Cloud Dancer decided to forget the vision and concentrate on the "time of trial."

The trials of the hopeful boys were taxing, strenuous, and not without a great deal of hardship. Much was required, such as fighting hand-to-hand with fellow braves both on horseback and on foot. They were to fight until only one remained unbeaten.

During the time of trial, the young candidates were also required to run a series of foot races up and down steep hills and sloping mountains. But by far the most rigorous test of all was the trial of fire and water. It was a trial which every one of the young men passed, but took endurance and determination. Oddly enough, the only one who had any trouble with this test was Cloud Dancer.

The trial of fire and water consisted of a contestant taking hot coals from a fire on one side of a river to the opposite side. Once there, the contestant was required to build a new fire with the coals. The boys were given three chances and after much pain and suffering, all of which proved the endurance and determination of each contestant, they passed. Perhaps the part of the test which made it most difficult was that each boy was required to carry his fire in his bare hands. His only protection was his training.

The trick to this event was simple and had been taught by each boy's father. First, one dipped his hands into the cool waters of the river and then dried them in the sand. Having a firm, heavy coating of sand on both hands, the boy then plunged them into the smoldering fire and filled them with burning embers. Even though they were thus protected, the less time the coals were in the boys hands, the better. That was why it was important to cross the waist-deep river as fast as one could. Upon reaching the far side, the embers were quickly coaxed into a new fire.

On the day of trial, all the other young boys had accomplished the test of fire and water with only a few having to attempt it more than once. Then it was time for Cloud Dancer to begin the ordeal. With his hands heavily coated and filled with red hot coals, he charged into the flowing river and made for the other side. However, as he crossed, he became aware of his glowing reflection. The golden bird had returned. Cloud Dancer decided to ignore it. Unfortunately, as he neared the opposite side, he was forced to stop and face a gathering crowd of gawking people who pushed and shoved to see the shimmering phenomenon. At first, the crowd only murmured and whispered, but as the shape continued to change they began crying aloud. Eventually the cry grew into near hysteria. Unable to prevent the image and with the coals burning his hands, Cloud Dancer pushed through the crowd to complete the test.

Upon reaching the opposite shore, Cloud Dancer built a large fire. The boy hoped he would be praised as his brothers had been. Instead, the crowd stood in silent awe, dumbfounded and afraid to speak. When Cloud Dancer stepped toward them, they drew back, then turned and ran away in fear. Few stayed behind to hear his explanation. Cloud Dancer felt very alone.

Much later that night, during the final ceremony, several tribesmen came to voice their concern to the leader about Cloud Dancer. They stated that the watery vision presented an evil omen and spoke of the eventual doom of the tribe.

After the older tribesmen had voiced their opinions, several others stepped forward with objections to Cloud Dancer's becoming a full-fledged Ndee brave. Already annoyed by his unusual hunting prowess and trapping skills, they now feared his watery curse. They suggested the boy be sent away for the good of the tribe. Still others were waiting to have their say, when the medicine man appeared at the council circle where the tribe had gathered.

"The vision of the golden bird was first shown to me many nights ago," he began in a rumbling voice. "It was not supposed to be revealed to anyone except the boy. You all claim to know what it means, but do you? The wind speaks with many voices, yet which of you can tell me when it foretells the rain or the storm? This fiery dream or vision has been brought before me by Cloud Dancer. I advised him not to say anything. Now you know why. You all saw his reflection and now voice concern. But I tell you that he is one of us and will bring fear to our enemies. The boy should be allowed to remain, with his vision."

"Cloud Dancer will stay!" announced the leader of the tribe, reassured by the words of the medicine man. "Tonight, as is our custom, the name of every young brave who passes the time of trial will be added to the ranks of our warriors. Tonight and forever after, Cloud Dancer speaks with the voice of a man."

Although the tribe was troubled by the leader's decision, the law of their tribe forbade them to dishonor it with further protest. Yet the fear of what they had witnessed caused them to have reservations. They decided not to talk to Cloud Dancer or his parents. The other warriors, too, had little contact with Cloud Dancer. They worked with him, but said little to assure him of their confidence or trust. In all, life became a series of hardships for

Cloud Dancer and his family. So much so that they planned to leave and go into the hills. That night the enemy from the north arrived on the outskirts of their village.

It was never quite clear how the invading tribe managed to get so close to the Ndee camp without being detected. What was later surmised was that they had traveled at night and hidden close by during the day. Whatever their secret was, they did take the Ndee camp by surprise. It cost the lives of two dozen Ndee warriors to halt the invaders at the entrance to the valley. Thousands of enemy torches flowed steadily towards the camp. Everywhere the cry of war was raised and the Ndee hurried out to engage it.

The great courage of the Ndee was their best defense. The leader, experienced as he was in war, stood at the center of his panicking tribe. Barking out orders, he soon had a strong line of warriors protecting the entrance to the camp. Because he knew they were most important to the survival of the society, the leader ordered the women and children to retreat to the river.

The screaming, fighting, and dying was so intense and loud that many could not hear the orders that were shouted to them. Sending a few runners back and forth, the leader was able to at last establish battle order. The conflict was so fierce that dozens died on both sides over a few feet of ground.

With his painted war club in hand, Cloud Dancer joined his brothers in the night fight and soon proved to be a great asset. The Ndee stubbornly held their ground, but it was uncertain just how long they could hold out. Again and again, the savage attackers surged against the human wall of defenders, and time after time were forced back. Still, they knew that the Ndee did not have as many warriors as they did, and they were confident of their eventual victory. With great persistence they hammered against the Ndee. When, despite their many dead, the defenders continued to hold, the enemy decided to retreat in order to regroup and charge again.

While the enemy retreated, the chief, thinking to escape the charge, ordered the tribe to cross the river in their canoes. But they quickly discovered that the swift waters of the river had risen while they fought and swept their boats downstream. The dangerous currents of the river were much too rapid for the women and children to cross unaided. Those who might have crossed were holding the enemy back at the entrance. The leader became certain that there was no hope. He pictured the death of the entire tribe. Either they would be killed by the enemy or drowned by the river.

The Ndee warriors awaited the next attack at the entrance to their valley. The women at the river began chanting prayers to their heavenly protector. The tribe was sure that death was just moments away. Then, at the beginning of the enemy attack, the medicine man was seen frantically searching among all the warriors. He found the warrior he was looking for, but took an unexpected arrow through his chest. Wounded, he continued to talk to the warrior he had selected, and the two left the camp together. The fighting went on more fiercely than ever before. Death was everywhere. Suddenly, amid the terrible fighting at the entrance to the camp, a runner from the river came to the leader with an urgent message.

The warrior was at breath's end as he gave the leader his message. All the tribe needed, he reported, was a short while and they would all be safe. Skeptical as he was of this information, the leader asked the warrior who had given him the message. "It was the medicine man," declared the warrior. The leader told him to go back and tell the Old One that he would get the requested interval.

The leader then ordered his braves to form a front and to hold back the invaders with their lives. The warriors soon created an impregnable wall which the enemy began pounding with their great numbers. Meanwhile the leader wanted to know why only a short time was needed and what would happen after that. He raced to the river to see for himself. Upon arriving, he was blinded by a glittering brilliance flying above the river. Staring with disbelieving eyes, he witnessed a marvel which would live in his mind forever.

There in the pitch black night, which the glowing torches illuminated spottily from the shoreline, the leader saw a magnificent golden bird with huge ivory claws flying high above him. In the claws, he saw groups of women and children being taken across the wide river to safety. Upon setting one group down, the great bird flew back across for another load. The people trusted themselves to this glittering apparition, and as they were lifted up and over, they cried out loudly their joy and excitement. When the last women and children had been lifted to safety, the enemy, who by now had broken through the defenders, arrived to behold the golden bird.

So terrified were they of the creature that many were trampled by their own terrified numbers. Many more were injured by the great wind caused by the magnificent bird's wings. Those who were left were quickly set upon by the remnants of the Ndee warriors and driven out of the camp. With the Ndee chasing them and the golden ghost flying above them, the enemy was completely driven away. There was much joy in the Ndee victory, but there was also sadness when the golden bird flew off into the night.

It took the Ndee people many months to resume their life of peace. When the year had come full circle, the summer hunt was given a new meaning. A special dance in memory of their fallen warriors was enacted, celebrating the creation of the Golden Eagle.

It was later recalled that when the women and children were being taken across the river to safety that night, and chanced to look down into the waters, they saw not only themselves, but the warrior, Cloud Dancer in full battle dress. It was he, they said, who had carried them across the river. Many years have passed, yet to this day the Apache Indians still celebrate the Golden Eagle in ceremonial chants and songs. The dance is still one most often performed at the beginning of the summer festivals.

The Legend of the Mountain Gods

In a deep southern region of the lower plains states, in a vast open area enclosed by the Black Mountains of California and the Great Bear River, near the Endless Sea, lies a ghostly place known to my people as the Ho-ka-ney, the Land of Perpetual Silence. Out there on the endless miles of scorching sands, amid blowing winds and treacherous creatures, exists an enchanting secret of the ancient Ndee. It is they who recall a centuries old legend, later changed into a timeless Indian chant. Among these desert dwellers, this song is very important as it deals with the origins of one of the desert spirits.

In the age before my grandfather's time, long before he related the story to me, there lived a mighty and powerful race of people who called themselves the Sa-Qua, which means People of the Spear. In ancient times, these spear people lived in the high mountains. Today, this same race is confined to one of the most forbidding and hostile deserts in the world. How this change came about is the heart of my story.

Long ago, wherever the desert peoples lived, they understood little of the spirit world beyond them. What they did know about, they explained in simple terms. To them thunder was the angry voice of the Sky Father, the wind was his breath, the white clouds were his dreams. His wife was known as the caretaker of their heavenly home, and when she was happy, she created the beauty of a perfect day. When she was sad she wept, and this was evident in the rain. It was she who gave voice to the song birds and color to the desert flowers.

The Sky Father created many races of people. The Sa-Qua were nearly twenty feet tall. For their protection, he gave them several sets of arms and armored their bodies in such a way that no mortal could touch them without being injured. He set them atop the highest mountains in the region and promised them his protection as long as they stayed near him.

Due in part to their near invincibility, the Sa-Qua became arrogant and insolent. They squabbled and fought amongst themselves and this made the Sky Father sad. Because they were armored and immortal, their spears would cause terrific flashes of light when thrown against one another, and their deep thunderous voices could be heard miles away, especially down in the valley near the home of the other children of the Sky Father. One of the many tribes which often heard the thunder in the far away mountains were the Ndee. They had always known of the mountain spirits and referred to them as mountain gods. The elders of the Ndee tribe taught their children that when it thundered high above on the snowy peaks, the mountain Gods were angry and were quarreling amongst themselves. Moreover, when they threw their sky spears at each other and missed, they often struck the earth below. To the Ndee, these sky spears were called lightning.

Each time the Ndee saw a lightning bolt flare across the heavens or come crashing down to the earth, they surmised the mountain gods were angry or perhaps someone had encroached on their spirit home. It was common knowledge that no mortal was allowed on Black Mountain where the Sa-Qua lived. To go there meant death. It was understood by valley inhabitants that nothing angered these mountain gods more than to have unwary intruders trespassing upon their sacred ground.

The majestic mountains were revered by the Ndee as special lands reserved for the spirits. They were supposedly inviolable. If someone broke this law, he or she would be pursued by the gods and killed. Thus, the Ndee, like other valley tribes were respectful of these highlands and were fearful when dark, mysterious clouds would appear.

When these clouds gathered overhead, the Ndee knew to take shelter quickly. They suspected these dark magical shapes hid the avenging spirits. If the clouds were seen atop the mountains, they concluded that the spirits had gathered to celebrate. The ensuing noise was the inevitable argument and eventual battle among the ever quarrelsome mountain gods.

Few ever visited Black Mountain. Occasionally there were reasons to go there, and those foolhardy enough to do so knew that the entire mountain was considered sacred. Unless it was a matter of life or death, no one would go there. It was common knowledge that if anyone dared to go beyond the snow-lined trees and up to the dark forbidden peaks, they would most likely die. And if someone wanted proof of the mountain spirits' vengeful anger and power, they had only to witness the murderous effects of an avalanche and the destructive trail it left behind. These awesome occurrences were usually caused by some wayward and unknowing stranger who had dared to venture onto sacred soil. The spirits usually warned only once; not often was there a second warning.

In the beginning of their history, the Ndee were a very peaceful race. However, in the course of time, due in part to many marauding tribes, they produced many great warriors. One such warrior was their chief.

The chief, while still in his youth, led his tribe to many victories over his enemies. He acquired his name from an incident which involved a huge bird. The immense winged creature swooped down into the camp one day and snatched up a playful child directly in front of its unsuspecting mother. With many onlookers screaming in panic, the chief, at that time a young brave, seized his father's bow and with a single arrow brought down the great bird without harm to the child.

After the incident, his name became Great Bow. Thereafter, he was chosen to become leader of his tribe and to marry the maid of his heart's desire. She was an astonishing beauty called Little Water Bird. From the beginning and for the many years to follow, they loved each other deeply. When she died, it left a great emptiness in his heart. The chief seemed to lose his will to live. One night, he heard the silent call of the mountain and felt that the time had come to join his lost love.

Knowing he would soon die, the chief asked the medicine man to come to his tepee. When the wise man arrived, the dying chief informed him that the time had come for a younger man to replace him. Since the chief had no son, and since there was no immediate candidate, the medicine man knew what he had to do.

He called for an assembly of the great Council of Elders and informed them of the chief's wishes. They charged him to seek a new leader from amongst the young men of the tribe and reminded him of the special qualities they sought, as such a man chosen as chief must possess the ability of true leadership. He had to be strong, courageous, and, above all, he had to have wisdom, for such a man would guide the tribe for the remaining years of his life.

The entire tribe was aware of their chief's serious condition and were filled with deep sorrow as his time approached. Yet they were also aware that such is the destiny of all. The men knew that once the old chief joined his spirit brothers, he would forever after live among the clouds with his beloved wife. It was readily understood that upon his passing, a new chief would take his place.

As was their custom, the Ndee warriors and the rest of the people gathered daily in their brightest ceremonial dress to sing the praises of the stricken chief. They reminded the wind and earth spirits of the chief's many victories and accomplishments. Inside the tepee, the aged warrior's heart soared with pride. He knew that even upon his death, his memory would live on. He lay quietly, content with his good and long life. Now he challenged the death spirit to come and fight him.

Meanwhile, the medicine man began the important task of finding and selecting a new chief from among the warriors of the tribe. Because of his patience and wisdom, he was trusted to find just the right man. The council and the dying chief knew full well that he would not choose a man for one reason only. The man he chose, would have to prove his worthiness in every skill, act, and situation.

There were dozens of young braves in the tribe, and with so many capable men, the medicine man's search would not be easy. During the days which followed, he looked upon all the braves closely and carefully. In each he sought a special combination which he knew existed in but one of them.

Among the eligible braves whom the medicine man studied were many with enormous strength and stamina, yet self-sacrifice was alien to them. There were those who were gifted with the stealth of the lordly puma, yet they did not possess the understanding of why it kills. There were others who fought fiercely like enraged bears, yet lacked the discipline of self-control. Some were persistent like the badger, yet did not understand futility. Some had courage, but not wisdom. Others possessed tenacity, but not compassion.

Many days passed while the medicine man went about his search. However, after observing many dozens of braves, none of whom had the qualifications he was looking for, he began to think he would never find the right man. None of the braves seemed suitable. Still he persisted. The tribe depended on him. If only, he thought, there was some way to have all these special traits exposed in the man he was seeking. Finally, he decided to journey to the sacred mountain to pray to the Sky Father for help in his difficult quest. This was not unusual, for many problems were beyond the sphere of ordinary men.

During the time the medicine man was gone, life in the Ndee camp continued as usual with the natural cycle of life; young men and women of the tribe fell in love with one another and married. One of these couples was destined to earn eternal fame though they were unaware of it. The girl was called Night Blossom. She was in her fifteenth year of life and was favored with charm, grace, and a radiant smile. It was rumored that her smile was so extraordinary, it could induce the sun to shine even on a cloudy day. The idle hearts of young braves quickened as she passed them. Many sought her hand in marriage. Yet even as the young men pursued her, there was only one brave who could quicken her pulse. His name was Standing Bear.

Standing Bear gave little thought to the medicine man's search for a new chief. There were many others who, he thought, were much more capable. He remained content to possess a single loving heart. He was youthful and had features which caused a stir among the women of his tribe. He was tall, dark skinned, and extremely strong. Coupled with these was wisdom. Yet, aside from a bride, he sought nothing else.

With his piercing green eyes and dark black hair, Standing Bear was indeed a handsome youth. When he hid his features behind a mask of war paint, he became an awesome and fearsome sight to behold. Like his chosen love, he was young. Yet even at seventeen he was already known for his swiftness, courage, and especially for his ability to wield a great stone axe, which he was seldom seen without. Heavier than most axes, there were scarcely two men in the entire tribe who could use it as effectively as he. Yet his own enormous strength did not compare with the enormous love he harbored for Night Blossom.

Among the Ndee, it was not unusual for a love-struck brave to make known to the maiden's father his desire of marriage. In fact, it was customary to bring gifts and other tokens of friendship to the tepee of the father and to make the father aware of the serious and proper intentions of courtship to his daughter. The father would then evaluate the man, his accomplishments, and gifts, and then decide if the man was appropriate and acceptable for his daughter's hand in marriage.

There were those who brought Night Blossom's parents a great catch of fish, just for the privilege of talking to her. Others offered beaver pelts and otter skins. Still others offered baskets of dried meat. Many were the suitors, and just as many were rejected.

The gifts offered to a maid's father were seen as the best a suitor could offer. They were given with the understanding that a suitor could then express openly his love for the girl in question. Night Blossom's father considered seriously the feelings of his daughter toward her admirers. But often, feelings were secondary. He believed that one day a brave would appear before him with great gifts and that this man would be the brave worthy of his daughter's hand.

Even though other braves brought splendid gifts and suitable offerings for a single smile, it was rarely ever given. Night Blossom would sit patiently and listen to the promises made by her suitors and in this manner she expressed her appreciation to the young men for their show of affection. Yet, the only time her smile was warmly given were the times when Standing Bear would offer her a single flower. This little gift was small in comparison with what other braves brought, but its simplicity was all that Night Blossom required. With her father's permission, she and Standing Bear would walk through the camp, convincing onlookers that they were a perfect couple. Other braves who were brothers to Standing Bear felt that he made her smile easily. They were well aware of his great love for her.

The braves of the tribe were not angry or jealous of Standing Bear. They knew it would require much more than a simple flower to win the hand of Night Blossom from her father. Not only was he responsible for evaluating all gifts, but he also had to uphold tradition. He sat on the Council of Elders and could not go against custom.

Days passed and the search for a new chief went without resolution. Furthermore, the courting of Night Blossom intensified. Everyone in the camp became very interested in the outcome of the two separate contests.

Finally, Night Blossom's father proposed to the council that one test could settle both questions. The council agreed and all of the braves of the tribe cheered the decision. Standing Bear was overjoyed. He knew his skills were a match for any other warrior. For the hand of his beloved, he would risk his very life and, if winning included the tribal leadership, then so be it.

That night as the council chanted prayers for their old chief, the medicine man's wife took sick, becoming gravely ill. She had been with her husband for thirty years and their love for each other was still strong. Upon his return from the sacred mountain, the medicine man used all of his power and knowledge to help her. Night after night, he sang to the night spirits. Despite his many hours of prayer and vigil, his wife grew steadily worse.

The tribal women who were attending the medicine man's wife believed that she could be cured, but only if she drank the juice of a very rare plant root. This rare herb, they said, did not grow in the hills or nearby forests. It could only be found on the snowy peaks of Black Mountain. When this fact was revealed, many grew pale and were visibly shaken. To obtain this plant that would bring a cure to the old woman, also meant risking death. It was perhaps too much for the medicine man to expect. However, the council was not without influence or wisdom. They decided to turn the emergency into a chance for love and life.

The council declared that the search for the cure would become the great test. Any brave who desired the hand of Night Blossom and the leadership of the tribe had to prove that he could retrieve the much needed herb. Whoever was successful in bringing the cure to the medicine woman would win both Night Blossom and become the new chief.

Before the warriors set out in search of the magical plant, a ceremony was held to appease the mountain spirits. The Ndee hoped to gain their good will by offering them prayers and chants. They begged permission to enter the sacred slopes and offered sacrifices, requesting the blessings of the Sky Father. In response to the tribe's efforts to appease the mountain gods, a great storm appeared and lashed out harshly at their camp. The medicine man informed the tribe that the mountain spirits were not going to allow anyone permission to venture onto their sacred land. He stated that the gods were warning everyone to stay away.

Yet, aware of the warning of the mountain spirits, one hundred braves, having prepared themselves in ceremonial dress, left their beautiful green woods, and began the long trek across the empty, barren plains. Foreshadowing the near impossibility of the quest was the great distance between them and the high mountain. In between the two points lay the immense expanse of the Endless Sea, miles of empty scrub, rocks, and formidable desert. It was this emptiness that was the true guardian of Black Mountain.

It took two days before the relentless desert sun began torturing the bodies of the braves. The punishing winds added the lash of driving sand. Like millions of angry whips of dried leather, it stung with merciless fury. During the day the scorching sun blinded their eyes, baked their faces, and burned their bodies. Many expired from the blistering heat. Many more died from the freezing nights. And then violent sandstorms appeared, taking the lives of twenty of the men.

The continuing miles of empty nowhere claimed the lives of nearly half the adventurous band. The lifeless place offered no pity or shelter, and day after day men continued to die. It seemed that weeks had passed, but in reality they were only in the fifth day of the journey. Still, the determined group pressed on.

The following day was especially cruel. It began with an overcast sky. This produced rain, but too far away to be of value to the desert travelers. Then, unexpectedly, they were struck by a flash flood. Ten men were drowned. In the afternoon they suffered from muggy humidity which later shocked their bodies with an extreme drop in temperature. To add misery to these harsh conditions, a great swarm of mosquitoes attacked and drove many to suicide with their ravenous appetite and merciless stings.

Still, the remaining braves pressed on. Already, the inviting contest was transformed into a struggle for survival. As they traveled, the winds ceaselessly thrashed them. The blistering sun scorched them, and the empty miles taunted them. Nowhere did they find relief. Moreover, their water supply was beginning to dwindle. The limitless plains showed nothing on the horizon and the burning sea of sand and rock offered no quarter to those who lagged behind.

Unlike their home there were no trees, no flowers, no bushes, no rivers, nothing! Only a limitless ocean of sand. An inferno of endless mirages, the vast desert awaited the living like a perching vulture. It seemed unconquerable. To the courageous, it was the greatest challenge of their lives. Ambition urged others of them on. For a few of the more noble, it was a chance to prove their worth as leaders. But only one among them struggled forward unaware of anything except the desire to save a life and win a heart.

By the end of one week, there were only twenty men left. They were a tired and exhausted group, but eventually they arrived at the bottom of Black Mountain, which loomed overhead from a towering height. The braves started upwards, and immediately the sky began to rumble loudly. It grew dark and the earth shook violently. Some of the braves lost their courage and screamed, running away in terror. Those who stayed instinctively looked to Standing Bear for leadership. Without hesitation, he grabbed his axe and led the way.

The Ndee warriors, having survived the punishing desert, were now challenged by steep and sheer cliffs which seemed to soar upwards beyond their strained vision. Many were too exhausted to continue, and decided to rest and to return home. Knowing it was important to go on, Standing Bear nevertheless stayed to care for his injured brothers before joining those who went on ahead. Hours later he caught up with the main group. They were struggling through a thick maze of giant trees. The braves found it difficult to proceed and many worried about the mountain gods they were likely to meet.

The night descended fast as the tired band finally came to the snow line. This white sheeted area reminded the Ndee braves that the trees marked the last boundary between themselves and the spear makers. A few of the more cautious grew reluctant to proceed until Standing Bear led the way. With the snow tugging at their feet, they trudged upwards. Then the air became noticeably thin and difficult to breathe. One brave suggested that the spirits were stealing their breath. Convinced of this terrible possibility, several more turned back.

Reaching a small, open area, Standing Bear stopped to take stock of the dwindling group. Only seven braves remained, and he urged them to follow.

As they walked, quite accidentally, one of the men stepped on a long dry branch, breaking it with his weight. The sound ripped the heavy blanket of silence with a thunderous echo. With incredible speed the clear snapping sound shot through the snow-covered trees, bounded off great boulders, and flew off into the snow-capped peaks above. Without warning a tremendous shock wave was felt and seconds later the ground beneath them shook, heaved, and trembled violently. Directly, there exploded a roaring avalanche, crashing down from above. With almost unrestrained power, the mighty avalanche crashed through, flattening trees, smashing boulders, and crushing everything in its path.

Two braves were caught in the rushing snow and were swept up and over with a swiftness they'd never encountered before. Two other braves were smashed by the monstrous, all-engulfing avalanche. These four were never seen again. One brave tried to outrun the wall of snow as it raced after him, but to no avail. One moment he was seen speeding down the mountain, and the next, he had vanished.

Perhaps it was instinct, perhaps fear. Whatever it was, it caused Standing Bear to grab a nearby brave and quickly dive underneath an overhanging cliff as the murderous wave of death roared over them. Minutes later, the scene was calm, leaving the two men to crawl up out of the snow. Standing, brushing themselves off, they paused to consider the option of turning back. A strange stillness fell upon the forest as the two tired warriors decided to rest. Standing Bear urged his friend to have something to eat. Collecting his thoughts, he did the same. Unable to think of turning back at this point, they both soon stood, took in deep breaths, and then climbed on. After expending considerable effort, they had passed the massive trees and were nearing the snow-packed summit.

At this great height, a mysterious green light lit the landscape. Stopping momentarily, they looked down and saw vast miles of clouds blanketing the land like an immense white carpet. Neither man could see the earth below because of the clouds and the strange mixture of light and darkness.

At the summit, the ground flattened out and there soon appeared a gigantic, arched gateway. The colossal doorway stood at the point where the mountain funneled into a most wondrous village. Cautiously they proceeded forward, through the portal, quite aware that the temperature had changed from freezing cold to pleasantly warm.

The two braves divested themselves of their heavy clothing and went ahead in their traditional loin cloths. Nearly fifty yards past the gate they approached the midpoint of a large stone courtyard which led into the dazzling village ahead. Suddenly, the pleasant quiet was shattered by a thunderous voice. "Why have you disturbed our land?" boomed the voice. "It is forbidden to violate sacred soil."

"My name is Standing Bear," answered the proud leader. "I have come..."

"We know why you have come!" the mysterious voice said, seeming to originate from everywhere at once. "Your troubles are not our concern. Because you have violated the law, you will pay with your lives!"

"Please spare us!" pleaded the other brave, falling to his knees in fear. "Forgive me. Please forgive me."

"Why do you not fall to the ground," asked the rumbling voice of Standing Bear, who remained erect. "Do you not fear death?"

"I will not die with shame in my heart!" responded Standing Bear, gripping his war axe and lifting his colorful shield. "I have not come to give my life, but to save one. But if that is your price, then come. I will do battle with you."

With loud raucous laughter, the voice all but forgot its purpose. "You dare challenge me to a fight?" the voice asked mockingly. "We are immortals here. No one has ever conquered us. We are invincible!"

"Then I shall be the first," proclaimed Standing Bear, still searching for the body of the voice. Everywhere he looked was the same, a thick shroud of glowing green mist. Except for his frightened friend, Standing Bear could see nothing. "Come, show me what you look like. I will not run. Are you afraid of me?"

"Ha!" the voice thundered angrily. "Then so be it! Look now on the power which will seal your fate. Prepare to die."

With his companion cowering on the stone floor next to him, Standing Bear's eyes opened wide, awed by the enormity of a gigantic man walking out from behind a thick veil of colored mist. For an instant, Standing Bear recoiled slightly. The giant man walked slowly and with only three steps stood directly before the two Ndee warriors. Standing Bear guessed that the giant was nearly eighteen feet tall. He was covered from head to foot with a luminous green skin; a round spiked helmet protected his face, and his body was armored from head to toe with small pointed spears. The giant stood silent, allowing the tiny brave to admire him.

Protected with such armor, Standing Bear concluded this warrior couldn't be touched by any opponent, much less held by him without injury. The giant continued to stand silent before him, grinning broadly as the astonished brave evaluated his opponent's potential. Standing Bear knew that this was no ordinary giant for, beyond all his other features, the enormous man possessed four arms, two of them holding lightning bolts. The brave on the floor, took one look up and fainted.

"Now do you fear me, little man?" asked the giant, with two hands on his hips, the other two threatening to throw his bolts. "My people are called the Sa-Qua, the spear soldiers. I am the warrior entrusted to guard the village gate!"

"I, too, am a warrior!" replied Standing Bear, gripping his war club. "I am surprised there is only one of you here. I have come to remove a special plant from your village. It is badly needed for my people. If need be, I will take it by force."

"I like you little man," laughed the giant. "Because you do not show fear, I shall allow you to fight me. If you win, you may go free. If I win, you will both die slowly. Do you agree?"

"Only if you will agree to let me take the plant when I go" added Standing Bear, "and my friend here."

"Why?" rebuked the giant. "Why do you bargain for the flea on the ground? He is not worthy to be in the company of warriors. But nevertheless, I will agree to the plant and also set him free if you win."

Keeping his eye on the towering giant, Standing Bear lowered his club to his side and took up a small pouch. While he loosened the top of the pouch, he asked his companion to rise and move to the rear. The brave did so instantly, but was curious as to why Standing Bear was not frightened of the giant. He also wondered why

Standing Bear had chosen to fight the immense warrior with a pouch instead of his war axe. Twenty feet from the two combatants, the frightened warrior stopped and watched as Standing Bear took up a defensive position confidently.

When he saw that Standing Bear was in position, the towering giant drew back a lightning bolt and threw it at him. At nearly the very same instant, Standing Bear dodged out of the way and threw up the contents of his pouch. A split second later the lightning spear and the pouch's contents collided in a huge explosion, creating an immense and blinding yellow fog. When it cleared, the giant looked about, searching for Standing Bear. He seemed to have vanished from the spot.

"Where are you?" demanded the baffled giant. "Come out and fight. I demand that you show yourself!"

Unknown to the giant, Standing Bear knew that he could never defeat such a well-armored opponent. The only thing he could do was to trick him. That was why, when the giant had thrown the lightning bolt, Standing Bear threw up a sack full of sulfur, blinding him. While the giant groped and searched everywhere, Standing Bear raced passed him and flew into the center of the mountain village. Although he was dazzled by the beauty of the surroundings, Standing Bear, nevertheless, searched for, found, and stole one of the rare plants that he was looking for. No sooner had Standing Bear seized one of the plants than another giant sounded the alarm signaling an intruder in the village. Scrambling from street to street, the agile brave sped away with a gathering crowd of emerald giants closing on his heels. Not daring to look back, Standing Bear ran for his life and soon found himself back at the main entrance to the village. Seeing the searching giant, Standing Bear took his great war axe and smashed the guardian's foot.

The giant screamed with a terrific howl as Standing Bear grabbed his clothes, axe, and his most surprised friend. Not pausing to talk, the two warriors sped past the giant archway and down the mountain. Back at the main entrance, the guardian was helped to his feet by a collection of Spear People.

Agreeing that their peace had been violated, the Sa-Qua took up their lightning bolts and called on young and old to follow the invaders and destroy them. To the last inhabitant, the spear people gathered at their main gateway. Suddenly, there came a great thundering from the heavens above them and a booming clear voice declared, "You are the children of the mountain. I have protected you from all harm while in my sight. But if you choose to leave my presence, you will loose my protection. Stay. Allow the plains children to go in peace. They have not harmed you in any way."

The Sa-Qua recognized the voice of their Sky Father. "We need no protection to punish these insects!" they responded angrily. "We will catch them if we have to chase them to the ends of the earth!"

"It is twilight here on the mountain," warned the Sky Father. "If you leave, you must return before dawn. Failure will condemn you to stay wherever dawn finds you."

The Sa-Qua shrugged off the advice as nonsense. Ignoring their Father's words, the entire group raised their spears in a war cry of death and soon after sped off down the mountain.

Because they were moving quite rapidly, Standing Bear and his friend were already three-quarters of the way down. Racing down the slopes, they did not dare to look back. However, because they were in such a hurry, they often tripped, slipped, and fell head over heels. In this fashion they flew down the mountain like two boulders.

Faster and faster the two fleeing warriors ran. Hardly watching where they were going, they half ran, half fell over each other, the rocks, trees, bushes, snow embankments, streams, branches, yet remained unconcerned about their injuries. Intermittently they could hear the roaring thunder chasing them and this caused them to ignore any safety precautions.

Unexpectedly they careened into an open clearing where a great sloping sheet of ice swept them off their feet and threw them into the air. Unable to control their trajectory or speed, they shot off into space and finished the last portion of the mountain flying through the air. With a resounding thud they struck the drift of the heavy snows at the bottom. The men who had waited behind dashed to dig them out. Taking a moment to thank his comrades and check the physical condition of his friend, Standing Bear wasted no time in explaining their danger. His one command came with such a serious tone, no one questioned it. Following his excited lead, the little band ran off into the moonlit desert.

All it took was one great roaring for the rest of the band to realize they were in the gravest danger. Hearing the thunder closing behind them, they increased their pace. It was perhaps the fear of imminent death that caused the braves to keep silent as they ran for their lives. As mile after mile fell behind them, one brave thought he might stop and rest. But one thundering footstep shaking the earth convinced him to continue his breakneck speed. Another brave curious as to the danger, stopped momentarily and peered into the darkness behind them. He saw the towering giants lumbering fast on the heels of the small band. That sight caused the brave to speed ahead of the escaping group.

The Sa-Qua had lived their entire lives in the high mountain clouds. They had never witnessed a dawn, but despite the Sky Father's warning, were not afraid of it. Besides, it was still night and sunrise on the plain was an hour away. It was impossible for the sun to rise any earlier, they thought. Thus they confidently concluded they could catch the thieves and still get back home before sunrise.

Once they reached the bottom of the mountain, their great giant strides meant that soon they would catch up to the Ndee who had, by this time, incredibly, covered half the distance back across the desert.

The great lumbering giants moved rapidly across the desert and were soon upon the Ndee. Seeing the tiny men running before them, they lifted their glittering spears and prepared to kill the fleeing men. Closer and closer they came until the Ndee did not have to strain at all to see the giants. Now the braves were certain they were going to die. Only the sunrise could save them, but that was still a half hour away.

Unknown to Standing Bear, Night Blossom had begun to worry about him. Despite the pleadings of her father she had begun a personal journey to see what was delaying her beloved. She braved the same dangers the warriors had suffered. Duplicating their journey, she paid the same price. But nothing except death would keep her from him. Now, as she fell exhausted on the plain, she knew she would die with the coming of dawn. However, as she knelt on the ground, she suddenly heard the nearing sounds of thunder echoing. Silently she waited to see what it was.

Out of the gray gloom came Standing Bear racing ahead of his fellow braves. The band looked terrified. But, unmindful of the sounds or her condition, Night Blossom saw Standing Bear, called him, and raced into his arms. Both of them hugged so tightly they nearly fainted. The other warriors, not caring if the two lovers had found each other an instant before their death, flew past them in sheer panic. The mountain giants were only a scant few yards away from their victims when the two lovers saw each other. The huge people were confident they had caught their elusive quarry and raised their multiple arms for the kill.

At the very same moment, Night Blossom's heart, excited by the sight of her true love, soared like a hawk regardless of the impending and vengeful giants. Just as their arms were raised for the kill, a smile illuminated Standing Bear's face causing Night Blossom to beam happily. In response to her beautiful radiant smile, the sun appeared, flooding the entire desert with brilliant sunlight.

Bathed by this early sunrise, the Sa-Qua froze instantly and were rooted to the ground. Unable to move, the giants' armor protected them somewhat, but as the light became more intense, the great spears of their bodies shrank into tiny stubby pins. The giants retained their enormous size, but they were no longer capable of moving about. Scattered throughout the vast desert, the entire race of giants was held solidly in place. None could move or speak. They were now like statues. In one last desperate attempt, their mighty arms lifted up into the sky to ask forgiveness from the Sky Father who, pitying them, gave them the power to store water to survive the scorching desert heat. But there they stood, and there they would remain forever.

As for the few remaining Ndee, they returned in triumph to their wooded hills. Once inside their camp, they gave the magical herb to the medicine man who cured his wife with a drink mixed from its powerful roots. Much later, Standing Bear was chosen to succeed as the new chief of the tribe. Soon after this, he married Night Blossom. Together they lived in great happiness.

Today, perpetual silence rules the mountain giants in the Endless Sea. Modern travelers through the place call the forbidding desolation the Mojave Desert. Through the ages the giants have lived and died. Today, they can still be seen standing there, holding up their multiple arms asking for pity from the Sky Father.

The race of people who were once called the mountain gods were changed into the Saguaro cactus. My grandfather once told me that they are still considered the spear warriors, and no one may touch them without injury to themselves. Interestingly enough, a flower grows on their spiny hides. Native Americans of the desert call it the Night Blossom. Curiously enough, it only blooms at sunrise.

The Legend of the Sky Brothers

There has always been mystery connected with the sky. In the early history of the ancient Indians, it was considered the realm of departed spirits. But it was not only the home of those who died; it was much more. Gazing upwards, the earthbound people often imagined what magical powers lived above them. The sky, with all of its changing moods and various temperaments, gave them not only a sense of majestic wonder, but also the belief that they were being observed and influenced by omnipotent powers.

Those mysterious sky spirits became an important aspect of many legends. The creation of sky myths stemmed primarily from the premise that everything living on earth had a celestial beginning. It was from that shadowed realm that a pristine source of power entered the virgin earth. Once there, it radiated and manifested itself with myriad purposes. It became the trees, forests, mountains, rivers, clouds, winds, insects, animals, fish, and birds. Once established, this sky force, the source of life, became a place to which all powers would eventually return. For the Ndee, this eternal source inspired and governed all ambitions.

It was the constant search for spirit power which compelled the Ndee. Their descendants, the modern Apache, still insist that without power, the spirit, or soul, cannot remain strong. One legend speaks of this spirit power and how it came to be. It tells the story of a sky symbol which, even today, reminds would-be warriors of their commitment to the search for power. This is that story.

Long ago, in the early years of history, there lived a
remarkable tribe called the Ndee. They were a simple
people. Their culture, society, and social structure all
were rudimentary. Within the tribe, men, women, and
their children had specific roles in life. To neighboring
peoples, however, these Ndee were anything but simple.
They viewed the Ndee as a formidable force with
superior warriors and hunters. They were in awe of their
womenfolk, whom they considered indomitable. But the
most outstanding feature documented by observers was
the impressive courage of the Ndee warriors.

Not all tribes were privy to this information. Some
marauding clans passing through Ndee territory
acquired it firsthand. Without knowing or caring who
the Ndee were, they attacked and made war on them
and tried unsuccessfully to steal their possessions and
children. They were shocked at the intensity of
retribution inflicted upon them by the otherwise peaceful
Ndee.

The attackers who escaped with their lives were
fortunate. Indeed, most often, the survivors returned
with humility, respect, and gifts to make peace with the
Ndee. When dealing with their counterparts, the Ndee,
like most other tribes, observed treaties with reverence
and honor. It was a tradition which served them well
until the Europeans came.

But in ancient times, when a people gave their word, it
was sacrilege to violate it. Thus the Ndee gained
prestige and power that forged a reputation which
spread across the deserts, plains, and mountain villages.
It began in the heart of their nation and was nurtured
through successive generations.

Where the upbringing and care of a child was concerned,
Ndee mothers and fathers became the wellspring of
tradition. Children were exposed to, and soon became
accustomed to, their particular social position and status.
In this society, everything and everyone had a place. As
people grew to maturity, these social mantles were not
only worn by them, but would dictate who they would
become as they aged.

Within Ndee society the differences in role or status were easily discernible. However, from a distance, their unique customs and traditions became the features by which others often recognized them. One Ndee peculiarity which stood out in ancient times was the curious tradition of painting the body. Not all clans did so, but those which did became defined by it and distinct from the others.

One clan which practiced the art of body decoration and design, or spirit illustration, was called the Painted Ones, *G'oshd'leezh'Ndee* or "Tintos." This particular group had a most interesting reason for their painting. They believed that their ancestors had literally arisen from the earth's interior. Because they venerated this earthly birth, they tried to embrace and emulate the vibrancy of the earth's natural colors and wonders.

The fathers, mothers, and their children carefully selected suitable shades or patterns and wore them proudly as signs of respect and honor. Among the tribe's many patterns were symbols such as the deer, bear, bird, tree, and so on. It was customary for the children to take their earth signs from those already worn by the parents and then add a variety of colors. In this way, other tribal members were able to recognize a particular member as belonging to a known family.

One family loved the earth so dearly, they chose symbols which they believed would tie them closer to her. The father, a proud member of the tribal council, was known as Two Suns, and his body image was a large red and yellow symbol which resembled the rising sun. The mother, an astonishing beauty called Bright Path, wore patterns which resembled leaves and were light green in color. Each of their four sons elected to follow his parents' example.

The eldest son was a tall, handsome individual whose feats of skill and courage were seldom matched by any other in the tribe. During his boyhood, his body illustration had matched that of his father. But when he took his place alongside his father in the council, he changed it to the brightest red hue he could find. His knife, bow, arrow, and even his great spear were easily identifiable at a distance. Because of his talisman he was called Red Spear.

The second brother, also tall, though slightly gaunt, was influenced by his father's wisdom concerning the sun. He was often in awe of its brilliance, which could easily blind the unprotected. He chose to paint his body bright yellow. His clothes, weapons, and shield were all designed to project the sun's powerful midday rays. So impressed were his friends that they called him Yellow Knife.

The third son, a brawny, stout-shouldered lad, was careful when he, too, took his place at council next to his elder brothers and father. His mother was a dedicated teacher of the earth's natural defenses. From her he had learned of the woodland colors and, after much thought, had chosen a combination of greens for his body design. It proved extremely effective. On many occasions, his friends, fellow warriors, and even his brothers were hard pressed to locate him if he hid in the forest.

In complement to his camouflage, he was named Green Turtle. It was apparent that, although other Ndee sons and daughters took to body painting and design, the offspring of Two Suns were the most popular. Thus it came as no surprise that when the fourth and youngest boy of Two Suns came of age, he too would be given a great name.

At birth, the boy was given the name Little Rain. As he grew to maturity, his passion for rivers and streams became an integral part of his life. He spent a great deal of time on the river banks watching the crystal blue waters snake their way through the spacious land. He loved the sound of the current and seemed possessed by its unbridled power and colorful majesty. He studied the river and sometimes even followed its course to the faraway headwaters, where the powerful tributary emptied itself over a towering waterfall.

The boy had reached the age of fifteen and by all accounts was a magnificent specimen of youth and strength. Although he was not as tall as his older brothers, many predicted that one day he would be. His mother considered him her favorite. He possessed her features and was a most handsome young man. His love and deep respect for both his father and mother, combined with his love of river waters, inspired his choice of color.

With his spirit touched by the magical river, the lad chose to paint his body a deep, rich blue. His shield, spear, knife, and clothing all were blue or tinted to that effect. Because of this combination and his wish to one day become part of the river, Two Suns renamed his youngest Blue Dancer.

Two Suns and his wife were extremely proud of their four boys. Wherever people gathered to boast about their children, few excluded the established merits of the children of Two Suns and Bright Path. Since the eldest three were members of the council, they took it upon themselves to instruct their youngest brother in the trials he would have to undergo in the days to come.

It was expected that every young man would become a warrior when he reached the age of fifteen. To accomplish this, he had to undergo several trials. They were all intertwined with the general spiritual beliefs of the tribe. Each step in its turn would cleanse the body of the youngster and expose the true nature of the emerging man. When the trials were completed, the boy would be a warrior in body, mind, and spirit.

The Ndee believed and practiced the art of metamorphic change for all tribal members. Children would learn proper behavior from their parents. The boys, up to the age of five, were taught respect and basic tribal manners by their mothers. At the age of six they were tutored in social responsibilities by their fathers. Detailed, specific behavior was taught by uncles and other close male relatives. If none were available, the boys were given over to a male guardian of a neighboring family.

For spiritual counseling, advice and general wisdom, they were usually supervised in a group by the eldest male tribe member. Often this was the medicine man. It was his task to see to it that each boy understood the spiritual bonding of tribal beliefs. The medicine man taught the boys the powerful workings of the spirits. He instructed them in how all living things originated and what powers the boys were able to harness from them. Through his teachings, the youngsters gained knowledge of power and their responsibility to acquire it.

The Ndee's shaman was a tribal elder named Medicine Lodge. No one really knew his age, but a good guess would have been near sixty. It was he who taught the young men the value of courage, and the disgrace and humiliation they would face if proven to be cowards. When a boy reached the age of fifteen, it was Medicine Lodge who schooled him in the importance of becoming a man.

The specifics of manhood included the arts of hunting and tribal warfare. In these arts, the growing boy was often taught through direct instruction and practical field experience. If he was taken along on a hunting trip, it was his job to care for the draft animals and maintain the supplies. Failure in these simple tasks was not only frowned upon, but quite often led to additional time among the younger students. In the oral report given by a senior warrior to a boy's father lay the fate of many a young aspirant.

The girls of the Ndee tribe were also given a specific role in life. Up to the age of ten, they were under the direct tutelage of their mothers. Further guidance was offered by older sisters, aunts, and other elder women of the tribe. If a young girl wanted specific knowledge in any area, it was often taught by the grandmother.

If the information sought by a young girl proved too specific for her grandmother, as often happened when dealing with ailments and their herbal cures, the inquisitive youngster was schooled by the matriarch of the tribe. In many clans this head woman was the direct counterpart of the medicine man. She was called the Den Mother, or Shama, *Bika'ge Shi'maa.*

The Shama's task was to instruct selected students in the medicinal arts. Her lessons were often as diverse as the lessons of an apprentice medicine man. Generally, however, the majority of a girl's education centered on her designated role in the tribe. Subjects such as weaving, sewing, cleaning, curing hides, grinding corn, and food preparation and storage were studied in addition to birthing and raising a family. If the young girl concluded that this knowledge was broad and intensive, the reason was that it was intended to be.

No Ndee girl having reached the age of fifteen was allowed to attain her metamorphosis and go through the magical change into adulthood unless she, too, underwent a rite, the ritual called the Corn Pollen Ceremony. In later tribes and clans, this ceremony became the main one by which the medicine man would confer upon the maturing girl the status of Changing Woman. Only after this passage was the young girl considered a full-fledged woman.

It was through special ceremonies like the Corn Pollen Ceremony that young Ndee children were allowed to become full-fledged members of the tribe. Before the ceremony they were treated as children. Afterwards, they were, for all intents and purposes, adults. This, then, was the kind of ancient rite of passage which the children of Two Suns had undergone. That is, all but one: Blue Dancer. His turn was nearing.

From the moment of their birth, parents of Ndee children were fully aware that their children were the promise of tomorrow. Furthermore, in ancient times, these same parents were given an opportunity to know the future. Not that they were given any special sight or forecast. Their opportunity came during the reading of names.

It was the custom of the Ndee to take one's newborn child to a special ceremonial gathering of the tribe. During the festive event, the clan not only acknowledged the birth of the infant, but requested the spirits to accept its tribal name and bestow a future on it. How this occurred was shrouded in mystery and included the Gathering Spirits, *Gan Gojitat.*

In the spring parents would prepare special gifts for the medicine man. It was into his realm they hoped to tap. In return for the gifts, the medicine man read the child's name into the roll of the tribe. Furthermore, each child was given a mystical prophecy as to what would be its destiny. In this way, the proud parents might have more than simply a common future to look forward to if they were informed by the medicine man that their child would bring them honor and pride.

Thus it was with Two Suns. As he and his wife watched each of their sons mature from child to adolescent to man, they noticed that all of them were bonding with one another more strongly than most brothers. The boys were seen playing together, working together, hunting, trapping, fishing and, often as not, fighting together. When matched against other boys of the tribe, they were a formidable group.

It was on the occasion of a buffalo hunt that the three older brothers took Blue Dancer on his first hunting trip. During the otherwise uneventful trip, they encountered a hostile group of neighboring warriors. In the ensuing conflict, the four brothers were observed battling with typical determination. Moreover, each displayed a concerted effort to maintain the safety of his brothers.

Even Blue Dancer fought as though he were possessed. Twice he was seen saving the life of Red Spear and Yellow Knife. Not to be overshadowed, the oldest brothers, too, showed that their love for their siblings went beyond the norm. Displaying flash and daring, Red Spear took an arrow meant for Green Turtle, and Yellow Knife saved Blue Dancer from a murderous club. In the final tally, other warriors of the conflict battling near the four brothers took it upon themselves to give Two Suns a detailed report of how loyal each brother had been to the remaining three.

This and other similar incidents made Two Suns and his wife extremely proud of their boys. So impressed was

Two Suns with the close adhesion of his offspring that he prepared a sizable gift for the medicine man. What Two Suns was curious to learn was why they had developed such a close-knit love for one another.

In the dark seclusion of his tepee, old Medicine Lodge went through a practiced ritual. It was an elaborate prediction ceremony which culminated in his asking the boys, who sat in a semicircle around him, to place their open palms into the ashes of a smoldering fire. Having done so, he then instructed them to hold each other's hands. Finally, he requested the two outer boys of the semicircle to turn their ashen outer palms to him. Then he spoke solemnly.

He told the brothers that their love for one another was very special. Indeed, it was unique. In all the land there would not be another such group of brothers for generations to come. Their future, he predicted, would be written across the sky. He finished his magical ceremony with the following decree:

"Separate you were born. Together you will depart. When your spirits bridge the world, we will see the joining of your hearts."

In what seemed like a prelude to the prediction, the Ndee had begun preparing a ceremony for the chosen boys of the tribe. However, when news arrived of an aggressor tribe having invaded their valley, all ceremonies were delayed. The aggressors' intentions were immediate and destructive. It was only the quick reaction of the Ndee chief that prevented a massacre.

The attacking tribesmen were called Che'lo'las, or People of the Night Bird. Their place of origin was unknown. Some speculated they had traveled up from the Land of the Vanished Spirit. But whatever their origin, their intention was never in any doubt. They had come seeking slaves and wealth.

It was no secret that Ndee clans were many. Their culture could be found scattered throughout the Southwest. But if one clan was living in close proximity to another, it was sheer coincidence. Consequently, when marauders or migrating tribes traveled through their land, the Ndee did not readily count on help from neighboring clans.

As it stood, when the invaders arrived, the Painted Ones numbered less than five hundred strong. The majority of the tribespeople were family members not accustomed to combat. Their warriors numbered perhaps three hundred. Still, what they lacked in numbers they made up for in skill and courage. These singular traits manifested and increased as conflict with other tribes became more frequent. As their lands dwindled and their personal losses became more heart-wrenching, the Ndee evolved into the most feared people of the Southwest.

However, in the ancient time, the Ndee warrior was only a shadow of what he would one day become. During this early, innocent period, Ndee warriors relied heavily on courage and the belief that the Giver of Life occasionally tested his children. Power had been given to them, and during times of war, they were observed to see if they were worthy of additional powers.

When the People of the Night Bird swarmed the Ndee camp, they were quite confident their numbers were more than adequate. It came as quite a shock to realize that although they had ten times the strength of the Ndee, they were being prevented from occupying the main valley area. The chief of the Night Bird People took to a high butte from which elevation he could observe the escalating battle.

From his lofty perch he saw that those whom he had attacked were a spectacular sight. Their brightly painted bodies blended in well with the magnificent plumed headdresses and colorful garb of his own warriors. The chief also noted that his warriors, despite their number, were at a disadvantage in the narrow vale. His main attack force was being checked by only a handful of painted warriors, but four of these soldiers were the most prominent he had ever witnessed.

From his high promontory, the enemy chief watched as, time after time, he sent additional detachments to flank the Ndee. Yet whatever his device, the end result was the same. The small but determined group that barred his way held, and continued to do so despite their dwindling numbers.

Desperate for some way to defeat the defenders, he discovered that the families of those who now fought against him had taken refuge in deep caves near the camp. Learning they were close to his position, he searched for them and, before long, he had the advantage he sought.

Word was sent to the valley defenders that if they did not surrender, their wives and children would be executed. In order to convince them, the head of their chief's wife was brought to the scene of battle. Seeing the great lady murdered, the defenders reluctantly dropped their weapons and complied with the surrender order.

In quick succession, the warriors were brought before the enemy chief, and while he gloated over his victory, the Ndee families were reunited and prepared to be murdered in like fashion to their chief's wife. This, however, was not the intention of the enemy chief. His joy in defeating such a valiant enemy made him want to savor his victory.

"I am Mo-qua-no, chief of the Night Bird Aztecs," he boasted, expecting cheers. When none arose, he began a long tirade describing his many victories against other tribes. In a wild, rambling speech before the Ndee, he praised his brilliance and skill as a leader. He boasted that his men would have eventually defeated the Ndee despite their efforts, because, he proclaimed, his followers were the bravest in the world. No one could match their courage.

Having learned his own chief had died in battle, Red Spear came forward and challenged Mo-qua-no to support his contention. Mo-qua-no was surprised that anyone would dare question him. However, he was curious. Was it possible that he had felt the sting of criticism? He sat up in his gilded chair and observed the solitary warrior standing confidently before him.

Mo-qua-no observed that the Ndee was painted from head to foot in the brightest shades of red paint he had ever seen. Further, the sunlight striking the colors gave the Ndee the appearance of being on fire. Red Spear's clothing, tribal markings, and even his feathered headpiece, were all shocking red. Had the warrior been dipped in flaming blood, the result could not have been more dramatic. Mo-qua-no was quietly impressed with Red Spear and having made a silent assumption, asked him if he had a last request before he died.

Undaunted by the threat of death, Red Spear repeated his challenge and dared Mo-qua-no to accept it. On behalf of the lives of his own people, Red Spear offered his own and dared Mo-qua-no to match his warriors against him in open combat.

Not intimidated by what he considered an empty threat, Mo-qua-no accepted Red Spear's offer and ordered his archers to kill Red Spear in place of his family. However, Yellow Knife rushed forward and said if Mo-qua-no was set on killing Red Spear, he, Yellow Knife would take his place. Mo-qua-no was stunned.

As the second Ndee warrior identified himself, Mo-qua-no's interest grew. "I am called Yellow Knife, brother of Red Spear," he said proudly. "I ask you to select one of your warriors to defeat me in any contest and see if the Ndee cannot match their courage." Mo-qua-no observed that the second Ndee was vividly painted in the most brilliant yellow sunbursts he had ever beheld. Large and small circular suns dotted the glistening, well-proportioned body. Yellow Knife's clothing, headdress and skin all flashed bright yellow.

Suspecting a pattern developing, as well as his own anger, Mo-qua-no believed more could be learned if he threatened to kill Yellow Knife. No sooner had he proposed it than Green Turtle and Blue Dancer came forward and stood before Mo-qua-no.

Side by side before the golden chair of Mo-qua-no, the four brothers stood defiant. They were a spectacular group, and even as they stood proudly together, each felt a special pride in representing his people before an invader. They all challenged the Aztec chieftain to choose any contest to test their courage.

Mo-qua-no took a close look at the four brothers. They all bore similar features, but their body colors made them distinctly different. Quite impressive, he thought. Asking that a drink be brought to him, Mo-qua-no demanded the two new arrivals' names. "I am Green Turtle!" announced the third brother, dressed in various shades and patterns of a woodland forest. "And I am called Blue Dancer," the youngest voiced proudly, his body paint matching the clear blue sky above.

Except for his youthful features, Mo-qua-no could not find anything which did not promote the youngest boy's fierceness. He may have been young, but Mo-qua-no was not fooled by his age. He was as much a warrior as the first three. With Red Spear at the forefront of the valiant brothers, the colorful group awaited the Aztec's decision.

Continuing to study them, Mo-qua-no suddenly realized that the four men who stood before him were the very ones who had prevented his victory in the valley. The conclusion that the four brothers had cost him dearly by causing the deaths of a number of his warriors, coupled with the fires of jealously and revenge stirring within him made Mo-qua-no proclaim loudly before the people of both tribes that these four would suffer the most horrible death he could devise.

Sitting quietly for nearly an hour, Mo-qua-no somberly considered many forms of death which might pierce the shield of courage these four men displayed before him. Yet all of his choices seemed puny and insignificant. At length he asked his advisors to suggest something hideous and terrifying. He needed something which would defeat the Ndee while exemplifying the might of his own men before all.

One of the advisors who had traveled through Ndee territory and was familiar with the land and its sights informed the chief of a monstrous waterfall only a few miles away at the headwaters of a great river. The advisor described how he had once seen a man fall from the ledges there. The poor victim, he related, smashed his body on the jutting rocks, then was consumed by the demonic boiling waters and drowned in a steamy whirlpool.

An inspired Mo-qua-o and all his captives made their way to the headwaters. It was a place where the river, which had snaked through hundreds of miles of open countryside, entered the interior of the mountain and emptied itself into a gigantic cauldron of death. Several hours after they had begun, the Aztec and their captives stood staring down into the magnificent, but murderous, falls.

Beginning at a dizzying height, the rapidly surging waters charged forward at a tremendous rate, shooting out over boulders and sharp rocks to plunge headlong into a deep black depth two hundred feet below. Upon impact, the churning blue-gray waters made a deafening, explosive sound. Everyone, friend and foe alike, stood in awe. A small, stony footpath could be observed just beneath the roaring waters. Spectators took one glance at the murderous display of raw power and trembled violently.

This was the place where Mo-qua-no would learn if the Ndee or his own men were truly the most courageous of all. Wasting no time, he ordered four of his bravest men to step out onto the stony footpath of the waterfall and make their way along its glistening, slippery rim to the opposite side. Tauntingly, he dared Red Spear and his brothers to follow.

As the eight chosen men stepped close to the edge of the roaring waters, they fell silent. For a long moment, no one said a word. What thoughts were in each warrior's mind were not easily detected. But what could be observed was the definite concentration each tried to maintain as he started across the narrow footpath which bridged the roaring river.

The contest would be one of sheer courage and skill, said Mo-qua-no. Those who survived the walk would be the winners. If the Ndee survived, Mo-qua-no promised to free his captives. If Mo-qua-no's men survived, the Ndee would become slaves. The younger brothers looked at Red Spear and remained composed.

Red Spear knew full well no one had ever completed the crossing. In fact, he had personally seen several of his own men fall to their deaths in previous attempts. No remains had ever been found. Still, with quiet composure, he accepted on behalf of his people. Respectfully he requested a word with his medicine man before beginning. Chuckling, Mo-qua-no agreed.

Upon his arrival, Medicine Lodge reminded the four of their destiny. It was quite apparent where they would meet their deaths. The four brothers spent a few moments with their parents and then proceeded to challenge the raging waters of certain death.

As Red Spear and the first of the Aztec warriors stepped forward along the ledge, the others held their breath. With the earth heaving, the ledge shaking, and the waters creating billowing clouds of fine mist, the Aztec warrior took a few steps, hesitated, lost his balance, slipped, screamed and nearly fell in. Red Spear caught him and helped him back to safety.

With the enemy warrior safe, Red Spear stepped confidently onto the narrow ledge, walked a dozen feet and was immediately swept away by tons of water. Without making a sound, he fell headlong into the depths and disappeared. Only a flash of red paint was seen streaking the frothy white current.

When the rest of Mo-qua-no's warriors saw how immediate and certain this death would be, they begged and pleaded with their chief to select another form of trial, as this one was impossible to survive. However, as Mo-qua-no began chiding his own men for their cowardice, the three brothers did not hesitate to follow their oldest brother into the falls.

The result was repetitive, immediate, and tragic. All three brothers were seen diving to their deaths with their individual color streaks following them. Not a single word came from either the Ndee or their enemy as they saw the silent deaths of the four brothers.

After a while, Mo-qua-no, truly impressed with the brothers' courage, freed his captives. He then asked the Ndee medicine man if anyone would remember their deed. Humbly the medicine man promised: "Only those whose hearts cannot touch the sky will forget. The brothers were born separate, but died together. Now they are bound by destiny to remain forever in the skies above our heads."

Mo-qua-no remained unconvinced until Medicine Lodge pointed to the mists above the waterfall. "Look there!" he shouted. "The four brothers will always inspire us with their unity and courage." Mo-qua-no, the Aztecs, and all the Ndee looked up into the misty sky and saw the bright colors of the first rainbow.[2]

---

2   In some versions of this story, the four brothers are seen being laid to rest by the Earth Mother in icy rock formations after their deaths. Thus their spirits can also be found in crystal cubes.

The Legend of the White Shield

Among the pages of ancient Indian lore are the sagas of the Southwestern Native American. These mystic stories evoke memories of a time when actual events became interwoven into the oral legacy of nomadic people. The legends were passed down from generation to generation through the custom of storytelling, and have become a wellspring of tribal songs and modern storytelling.

The storyteller, specifically selected by the elders in most clans, are the caretakers of a tribe's oral heritage. Accordingly, when he or she is entrusted to possess this special knowledge, a mystical and ancient bond unites them. Indeed, no students may consider themselves worthy to safeguard sacred information unless they have been selected by an elder or spirit representative of the tribe.

In some tribes of the Southwest, this selection is always made from the third generation in a family. Many speak of it as "preordained by the spirits." They offer as proof the traditional bond which manifests itself in the early years in the relationship between children and grandparents. Many outsiders question why sons and daughters are not the immediate choice. Sometimes they are, but more often it's the grandchild.

It has been suggested that in nuclear or traditional families, parents are often unable, due to their full-time duties, to educate their children in depth. As a result they easily depend upon a grandparent. This situation has advantages for all concerned.

In the basic social structure of many early Native American tribes, a grandparent, or in some cases an elder, would oversee the instruction in specific areas of a promising child. This instruction would allow the youngster to become not only a functioning representative of the tribe, but often an integral and vital part of his cultural community.

The knowledge which an elder might offer a grandchild could involve any number of important subjects. Tribal mysteries ranged from spiritual enlightenment, to philosophy, to healing taught by the medicine man, or shaman. Additional skills or applications could be supplied by the curandera, or medicine woman. Rare cases might even involve learning tribal mythology. This would be the realm of the storyteller, Ni'a-la'go, or Vejo Estorio, who would be the source of the oral traditions and heritage of the people themselves.

Such was the case in the legend of the first storyteller. He was born to a clan which called itself the Spirit of the Black Shell. Among them lived a loving couple who became the proud parents of an infant born during the first recorded lunar eclipse. When the moon reappeared, the image they saw in that celestial neighbor was that of a walking bear.

In ancient times, tribal communities put great stock in apparitions that accompanied the birth of any child. Moreover, children born during unusual sightings or occurrences were often thought to be a curse or a hindrance to the tribe. The interpretation of birth omens was left to the shaman, or medicine man. The spirits gave him the power to decipher these clues.

It was the custom of the ancient Ndee to present the newborn to the tribe in a special nighttime ceremony called the Gathering of the Gan, or spirits. On this solemn occasion, the infant's name was proclaimed aloud before the assemblage of the tribe as they chanted and danced around a huge bonfire.

If no natural phenomenon occurred, or "replied," to spoil the ceremony, the child was said to be accepted by the spirits. However, if a reply was heard, it meant that the spirits were concerned or angry and the child should be killed, banished, or chastised in some manner.

The parents of the infant born during the night of the eclipse were considerably worried about the bonfire ceremony and the fate of their son. Hoping that the image of the bear seen on the face of the moon was a good omen, they named him Walking Bear. Nevertheless, they were apprehensive the night they brought him to the nocturnal gathering. Like other parents, they anxiously awaited the decision of the medicine man.

The evening ceremony got under way, and nothing out-of-the-ordinary happened. When it came time to offer Walking Bear's name to the spirits, the clarity and bright sheen of his namesake, the moon, was interpreted by the medicine man as a good sign. Relieved, his father and mother celebrated with the rest of the happy tribal parents. The celebration lasted until dawn.

Few people were aware that the medicine man always revealed only half of what he knew at the ceremony. It was his prerogative to protect the innocent from the fearful. Had he announced that the boy would one day grow up to dance with the spirits of the dead, the tribe might have found reasons to dislike the child.

Protected by the silence of the medicine man, the child grew to boyhood and easily mastered his woodland skills. By the time he reached his sixteenth birthday, Walking Bear was a match for any boy his age. With considerable respect for the teachings of his parents and elders, he personified those honorable traits expected of every Ndee boy.

From his father, he learned when to show courage and when to show discretion. He learned of the respectful customs pertaining to married and single women of the tribe. From his mother he acquired bearing and nobility. Walking Bear learned well.

Day after day, Walking Bear continued his studies. From the hunters of his tribe, he learned how to track the elusive desert animals. Like most boys his age, Walking Bear was anxious to prove he had mastered the arts of stalking and evasion as well as every other skill he had been taught. Information swelled within his head and he needed an outlet.

On one of the first clear days of spring, the chief called on the hunters of the tribe to prepare for the annual hunt. It was customary during the late winter and early spring to choose hunters to journey out to meet the returning herds.

It was common practice for the chief and his warriors to hunt. During most of the year, this was a weekly chore for all families. However, due to the hardships of winter, many households had depleted their winter stock of supplies and were anxious to feast on fresh meat. Once winter began to exhibit signs of evolving into spring, the tribe anticipated the return of the buffalo, elk, and mule deer to the open plains, which prompted the spring hunts.

Each of the several hundred hunters of the tribe was hoping to be selected for the main expedition. Much honor and power was to be gained by leading, or at least being part of, one of the many hunting parties. Those selected could always count on being honored and respected for participating in this fashion.

It was no surprise when only the most experienced scouts and hunters were selected by the chief. His decisions had a profound effect on the tribe's conception of his ability to recognize good qualities. Furthermore, his own physical leadership and experience were reinforced by leading the main expedition. The mission was simple. He and his men would search out and hunt the returning animals.

As it happened, Walking Bear's father was one of the experienced hunters of the tribe and was honored by being selected by the chief. In times of necessity or training, it was customary for young sons to accompany their fathers on such a hunt. That not being the case, Walking Bear and several other hopefuls were requested by the chief to remain as reserve guardians of the camp. This in itself was also an honor. Walking Bear was proud.

Depending on the weather, the expedition's travels could take them to the far horizons of the desert or even to the distant lofty mountains. It was not unusual for hunting parties to take several weeks to cover a vast amount of territory in their search.

With a great deal of commotion and fanfare, the hunting parties were gathered, divided, and dispersed. The chief and his hunters advised their families that they would return within twenty days. Because they would be gone so long, many of the women decided to conserve rations, space, and labor. Some households were combined, and others were merged according to age. The children stayed with their mothers, while young men and women came under the direct control and tutelage of their grandparents.

It was decided that during the hunting season, Walking Bear would live with his grandparents. His grandmother was a kind and gentle old woman named Turtle Woman. She was a practiced medicine healer whom the tribe regarded as invaluable in the arts of natural cures and spells. She taught Walking Bear how to protect himself against a number of ills, wounds, and witchcraft.

In addition to his grandmother, there was Walking Bear's grandfather. The wise one, as Walking Bear would remember him, was called Snake Circle. He possessed a quiet intelligence which allowed Walking Bear to realize that there was a great power behind his aged eyes. Walking Bear was also aware that his grandfather was a highly respected elder of the council and the keeper of tribal spirits.

Receiving him into their home, the grandparents began instructing Walking Bear in their respective fields. In the weeks that followed, Walking Bear learned of the birthplace of his ancestors. It was their spirit power, informed Snake Circle, which gave Walking Bear's grandmother the power to heal. All the memories of how their ancestors had journeyed across the land were locked in the stories of the ancients. Turtle Woman told him, "Your grandfather will teach you all of them. He has chosen you to carry them to the spirit of the dead."

Since coming to live with his grandparents, Walking Bear had absorbed a great deal of knowledge. He now knew how to safely remove porcupine quills, cactus needles, and bee stings with honey and turtle oil. He also learned how to communicate with the animals by tasting the wind. He learned how they were created and why the sky thundered when clouds danced across the blue ceiling.

Moreover, the ancient knowledge of how his ancestors acquired fire from the dark spirits of the underworld was his. He learned how man was created with a thunder rock and how the fox lost his ability to fly. He now knew why the color blue was sacred and why some fish were forbidden to be eaten.

Each night his grandfather told him stories, such as how man was forbidden to sleep in the sky and why women could never again use the surface of the sun to cook. The powerful knowledge of the useful and poisonous plants, flowers, and herbs of the woods was given to Walking Bear by his grandmother. Both his grandparents were vast resources of information and Walking Bear thought that there would never be enough time to learn it all. Still he owed it to the memory of his ancestors to try.

The wisdom his grandparents had accumulated in their eighty years was small in comparison to the amassed information of his tribe. With diligence and perseverance Walking Bear resolved to learn as much as he could. He was proud of what he knew, but sorry he had not learned it sooner. Incidental to his new wisdom came the prestige of being the apprentice of the storyteller. This earned him respect and great honor.

When in the course of ten days no word had been received from any one of the hunting parties, no one in the village was concerned. However, when the cold weather which had been expected to diminish stayed and began to grow in strength, the village buzzed with worry. It was unusual for spring to be late; perhaps the sky spirits were angry.

The medicine man was consulted. He entreated the spirits and advised the people to prepare for a longer winter than expected. This information created uncertainty about the expected return of those who had gone on the hunts. Owing to the prediction of a prolonged winter, runners were sent to the hunting parties. But after another ten days, none of the runners returned. The failure of the chief, the hunters, and now the runners to reply or signal their whereabouts caused alarm among the families who waited in the village.

A special meeting of the governing council was convened to discuss the options of the tribe. Since the chief was away, the Council decided the eldest member would preside in his place. It was a temporary honor, but one which was warranted. The elders talked, smoked, and debated for hours. In the end, it was decided that new search parties be organized and sent out after the missing groups. There was concern that there might be an insufficient number of experienced warriors for the task.

It was decided that, due to a serious shortage of men, the sons of the missing fathers would be allowed to accompany the remaining reserve warriors. Walking Bear took his leave of his grandparents and joined the twenty-five others who had volunteered to go. By design, the group was divided into smaller groups of five. Each group consisted of four young men and one experienced guide.

Walking Bear and his group were led by a warrior named White Tree. He suggested they go westward toward an area known as the Ribs of the Earth. That was the last known direction of the tribal chief and his men. With little else to go on, the group agreed and set off. So as not to lose sight of one another, Walking Bear and the others followed closely. Walking with grim determination, the rescue parties soon disappeared into the encircling arms of an approaching winter storm.

Spring had definitely arrived when the annual hunt had begun, thought Walking Bear. The sun had been shining, and the weather had seemed to be the advance guard of a wondrously warm season. Now it had changed dramatically. The sun was blocked by menacing clouds. Slowly trudging through the knee-deep mantle of snow, Walking Bear could not believe what he was witnessing.

Winter had returned and was blanketing everything to the horizon with a solid shroud of heavy snow. Following close behind the others, he could hear their footsteps crunching the deep snow. As the miles began to accumulate, and the snow storm increased in intensity, Walking Bear was unmindful that he was failing to keep pace with his comrades. As a result, White Tree and the others outdistanced him. In fact, he lost sight of them and was soon lost.

Feeling the stinging whips of the wind-driven snow on his face, Walking Bear was compelled to enclose his head in the warm coat which his grandmother had given him. He continued to walk blindly with occasional peeks from his hood to see ahead of himself, and when he did look, his own vapor obscured his vision. Finally, he felt exhausted and came to an abrupt halt. As he listened he instantly realized he was alone. Walking Bear stood absolutely still. Surprisingly the storm abated. In the temporary silence, he noticed that the emptiness devoured all other sounds. All he could hear was a lone wintry wind singing melodiously. Concluding he was lost, Walking Bear considered retracing his steps. But when he turned to retrace his path it, too, had disappeared.

Unsure of his position, Walking Bear pushed back the furry hood protector on his coat which shielded him. He estimated he was several miles from the tall mountains in the distance. In front of him, a heavy fog undulated like a great wave. Briefly it allowed him to view his surroundings. All around him, the snow and sleet had obscured any remaining traces of his companions' trail. He could not see the stars or the sun. This did not frighten him, but it did make him pause to consider what to do next. Walking Bear decided to go toward the mountains.

As he started off again, Walking Bear noticed that the snow began falling again. In fact, the faster he walked the faster it fell. It amused him to think he was influencing it. He decided to run. As he gained momentum, the storm returned and with it, the wind. It lashed out furiously and forced him to retreat inside his great coat.

Walking Bear couldn't see where he was going and several times he fell forward with great force. He decided to slow down considerably. His entire body ached from his effort, and the chill in his bones had become severe and painful. Shrugging off the accumulating fatigue, he thrust himself forward.

Walking Bear found that he could push on, but with great difficulty. Finally, feeling himself drained of energy, and unable to continue despite his best efforts, he stopped. Instantly the snow storm vanished leaving behind a foggy gray curtain. A light wispy sprite appeared and began playfully dodging about his head and ears like a wind dancing to invisible music. Walking Bear knelt down on the snow and rested, staring at the fog. The wisp nipped at his nose.

Ignoring the mischievous pixie, Walking Bear doggedly searched the fog for his friends, but he could see nothing. The wisp raced away, but soon returned. As it neared, he tried to catch it. Evading his hand, it retreated and came to rest a few feet from him. The glare of the white snow prevented Walking Bear from focusing clearly. However, as he concentrated on the steamy outline of the wisp, it hissed angrily and coalesced into the distinct outline of a human figure.

Suspecting he might be dreaming, Walking Bear rubbed his eyes repeatedly while looking at the steamy cloud. A solid form was taking shape, and unexpectedly it glided towards him. Quickly he stood lifting his axe, although he remained unconvinced of the being's reality.

Walking Bear hoped it might be a friend, but he was nevertheless prepared for an enemy. When the floating apparition ignored numerous requests to halt, he bristled. The war axe was drawn all the way back, ready to strike. His grip tightened as the figure drew ever closer. Eventually a distinct figure emerged from the mists and stood before him.

Walking Bear grew pale. He could clearly see that the phantasmic figure was a beautiful girl. She appeared very young, and wore little about her symmetrically perfect body. He shivered violently, wondering if it was due to the intense cold or to her dynamic appearance. Of one thing he was sure, she was no ordinary being. When at last she touched him, the strength in his arm waned and his axe dropped heavily to the ground and pressed its outline into the snow.

The wondrously beautiful girl remained motionless and Walking Bear felt a strange power began to envelop him. He sensed it was she who was somehow causing it. He was careful not to exhibit fear or uncertainty as he studied her in thoughtful silence. In all his life, Walking Bear had never seen anyone like her. There was something magical in everything she did.

Walking Bear guessed her age and stature approximated his own. The girl's youthful features were complemented by her beautiful attire and she had exquisite oval eyes. The list of her attributes was long and included her long black hair which was tightly braided and fell on her exposed shoulders.

Walking Bear traced the design of her finely sculptured hands, and gazed at her tiny feet, which were sheathed in handsomely crafted leather boots. The bright yellow leather hugged her ankles tightly and rose up to touch her knees. All in all, her majestic stance and attire presented Walking Bear with the unmistakable impression that she was a princess.

After staring hungrily at the young woman for several minutes, Walking Bear concluded that her garments would have allowed her to easily blend in with his people. One trait which Walking Bear selected as most appealing was her radiant smile. It caused Walking Bear's look of stoic caution and suspicion to be replaced with one of obvious delight. Her non-threatening demeanor allowed him to relax. He wondered if he should trust her.

Walking Bear had been intently schooled by his grandparents in the subject of spirits. They had diligently taught him about their special powers. It was due in part to these instructions and warnings that he knew that the girl was a spirit. He recalled that these beings were far from predictable. Some were peaceful and benign, others warlike and treacherous. Some were children of eternal powers, while others were merely apparitions seeking love, revenge, or simply understanding.

Whatever this snow spirit's purpose was, Walking Bear remembered that he had to be prepared for nearly anything. Collecting his wits, Walking Bear decided that although the girl was an extraordinary sight, if he wanted to live, he should hasten to discover her purpose.

The girl saw determination replace the smile on Walking Bear's face. However, she continued to smile and without ceremony, drew away and began to circle him. Walking Bear watched curiously as she danced with glad abandon in ever wider circles. While she danced to invisible drums, he recalled the advice of his grandparents who had warned him that spiritual beings could be erratic.

"Spirits can bring great changes to the weather," warned his grandmother. "If ever you see one, be aware of the earth and her moods." Recalling the advice, Walking Bear noted that ever since the girl appeared, the white snowy landscape had produced no sound. Aside from her steamy arrival and his own breathing and the occasional mush of the snow as she danced, there was not the slightest noise. It reminded him of a burial ground.

In addition to his grandmother's advice, Walking Bear recalled his grandfather's warning that spirits could alter their shape. They could even hide themselves inside natural surroundings, bodies of people, or animals. Was this girl really what she seemed to be? He had already noted she was oblivious to the biting temperature and knee-deep snow. Moreover, he wondered if she was aware of his thoughts.

The girl was making her fourth circle around his position when Walking Bear spoke to her. Because she did not stop her dancing, he was forced to pivot and follow her movements. "Who are you?" he asked.

"I am known as Odi'Li," she responded, flailing her arms about imitating a bird in flight. "Who are you?"

"I am Walking Bear," he answered with considerable dryness in his throat. "I am the son of..."

"I know who your parents are," she interrupted. "I want to know who you are. Tell me who you are," she said.

"If you know my parents, you also know I am a warrior. We are the Black Shell clan." His eyes following her as she circled. "We live in the shadow of the Ribs of the Earth. Tell me Odi'Li, what are you doing here?"

"I am looking for a shield," she said, finishing her dance and coming close to him. "Have you seen it? Have you seen my mother's shield? It's lying about someplace."

"What does it look like?" he asked stepping away.

"Do I detect hesitation in a warrior?" she giggled.

"I do not fear anything mortal!" he replied defensively. "But you are a spirit. I must respect your power."

The girl studied Walking Bear's eyes. They were solid green orbs and she saw no hint of fear in them. In fact, as he replied to her questions, she detected no fear in his words either. The slight hesitation she did notice, she attributed to her close proximity to him. Amused by his discomfort, she moved closer until their bodies nearly touched.

"My sister awoke a few weeks ago." She began gently running her smooth hand over his face. "She told me that I had better hide from the wrath of my brother. I hate him!"

"Your brother?" Walking Bear repeated, puzzled. He enjoyed the feel of her touch, but it was soon followed by a slow numbing sensation. A brilliant fire flamed in her eyes when she mentioned her brother.

"My white shield is the only protection I have against him!" she said, examining his great coat. "With my shield I can evade my mother's orders to stay with the dead, and can dance with you as long as I wish. You like my dancing don't you?"

"Yes," admitted Walking Bear, wondering why his coat felt heavy, wet, and icy cold. "I like your dancing very much."

"You are nervous, Walking Bear," she accused him, returning to look deep into his eyes. "It is not fear, I detect, but concern, worry. Is there something wrong?"

"I do not know what you want Odi'Li," confessed Walking Bear, returning her piercing gaze. "But there is a disturbing force in your beauty. I sense that I stand in a grave. I do not know why you have selected me, but I suspect when you have finished your game, I will die."

"My game?" Odi'Li repeated, taking his hand and holding it tightly in between hers. "Whatever do you mean? I told you, I'm only seeking my mother's shield."

"You spoke of hatred for your brother also," Walking Bear reminded her, his hand completely numb and in pain. "I believe your mother's orders, your father's absence, your refusal, and your brother's anger are all related."

"You are a perceptive man," Odi'Li concluded with a wide smile. "You are worthy to come and live in my house."

"Is there a choice on my part?" inquired Walking Bear.

"Unless you can prove you are of value to your people, I shall take you with me. My mother will allow me to take anyone from any tribe to my home. I have many in my possession now, but none are as handsome and pleasing as you are."

While she spoke, a new awareness swept over Walking Bear. He felt he was being protected from afar. The feeling imbued him with courage, and helped him to overcome Odi'Li's subtle magic. It was as though the girl's power was being kept in check.

Walking Bear suspected that Odi'Li's beauty was a lure. He sensed a darkness filled with death. If the signs were correct, he would soon meet her brother. "I suspect my father and all my brother warriors are with you," offered Walking Bear confidently.

"It is within my power to let you join them," Odi'Li informed Walking Bear. "Unless, as I said, you can prove to me that you are important to your people. Do you have a position of such importance? Are you necessary?"

"Is this a requirement placed on you by your mother?" asked Walking Bear. "That you may not kill anyone who has been selected and given a special purpose by the Giver of Life?"

"As I said earlier," continued Odi'Li, "you are very perceptive. That is the rule of my mother and father. But again I ask, do you have any special purpose or mission?"

"Yes," offered Walking Bear proudly and pointed to an area of snow where the two of them could sit and talk.

"Tell me what it is!" Odi'Li demanded. "I must know it. If you speak the truth, I shall allow you to go unharmed. If not, you must accompany me. Agreed?" Odi'Li took her place next to him on the snow bank.

Walking Bear nodded his head in agreement and said, "I am a storyteller. A keeper of secrets."

During the next few hours, Walking Bear told Odi'Li many stories. He regaled her with deeds of courage and entertained her with myths and magical transformations. He filled her heart with a variety of love stories which induced her to weep. Through all the wondrous adventures of his people, Odi'Li was able to feel their unselfish heroism. He told her of his people and their pride in their families and of their abiding love for nature and all her beauty.

Walking Bear spoke of the legends which recalled the journeys of the elders. He explained that the older one became in the tribe, the more honorably one was treated. He sang of the bond his people had with the Sky Father. Walking Bear ended his narration by describing the unselfish roles of the women of his tribe. He praised their enduring patience and unique relationship with Mother Earth.

When Walking Bear reached this point, Odi'Li became uncomfortable and stood up. She seemed to be hiding tears. Rising also, Walking Bear noticed the fog lifting in several places. The thick clouds were being swept aside by an invisible hand. Then, without warning the bright sun appeared and Odi'Li immediately caught fire and screamed in agony. In the next few minutes, Walking Bear saw her change from a ravishing beauty to an old woman caught in the grip of torturous pain.

"Help me! Help me!" Odi'Li screamed, writhing helplessly on the ground. "It's my brother and he's destroying me! Help me! Use my mother's shield to protect me, please!"

The terrible high pitched screaming shattered Walking Bear's calm and caused him to fly to where Odi'Li was spinning on the ground. With great urgency and speed and with as much force as he could muster, Walking Bear scooped up handfuls of snow from the ground and began covering her body.

The yellow sun was causing Odi'Li's body to melt rapidly and Walking Bear saw how extremely painful it was to her. Scrambling all around her steaming body, he raced to cover her. As she disappeared beneath the mound he had created, the wind returned and pushed the clouds back across the face of the sun.

With the sun blotted out, the screaming stopped and once again silence returned to the desert. Moments later,

Odi'Li reappeared. She was young again and did not look any the worse for the wear. Walking Bear smiled. She returned his smile and came close to him asking, "When did you discover how to use my mother's shield?"

"My grandparents!" said Walking Bear proudly. "They explained your duty to cover all things in winter with your mother's white shield. I know of your brother, the sun warrior. It is his fire shield he carries across the sky each day. My grandparents told me you are also called Woman of the River," said Walking Bear. "You are daughter to Earth Mother and walk with the spirits in the Land of the Dead. Your twin sister is Woman of the Spring. What will happen now?"

"I will return home without you!" she confessed sadly. "I must rejoin the spirits of the dead. But I will return in the winter. Promise me Walking Bear, promise that when you see my white shield lying across the land, you'll remember me."

"Only if you promise to release my father and brothers. And," added Walking Bear, "release your sister."

"Agreed," Odi'Li replied, beginning to disappear. "They are at your camp waiting to celebrate your victory. My sister returns tomorrow. May your children remember our story."

Upon joining his people, Walking Bear learned that his father and the rest had returned with a great bounty. During the festival which followed, he was informed that his grandparents had seen him in their dreams and reached out to protect him. When Walking Bear related his story, the tribe praised him. From that day, the role of the storyteller was placed among the highest positions of honor in the tribe.[3]

---

3   In some southwestern clans, the choosing of a storyteller is marked
     with celebration. During the ceremony the individual is sprinkled with
     white ash, or bones of the dead. This is done in remembrance of the
     trial with Odi'Li, Snow Woman.

The Legend of the Eternal Prayer

The spiritual center of the White Mountain Apache tribe is located on their reservation in Arizona. It is called Sacred Mountain. By its very locale, it is an exclusive and revered source of power. To outsiders, it is only a white-capped peak in the majestic Rocky Mountain chain. But to descendants of the ancient Ndee, this venerated summit, which towers over the southwestern continent like a colossal sentinel standing guard over their land, is the source of all their power.

The land of the Southwestern Apaches consists of a gigantic open range which once extended from Canada to Mexico. But however far the veins or routes of travel are measured, the heart of their territory still continues to pulse from within the Sacred Mountain. Here beneath the shoulders of the alpine tower exists a special piece of land which figures prominently in an ancient legend.

The area itself is not unusual, but what makes it remarkable is a large section of dense black forest which carpets the surrounding landscape. It measures approximately five million acres in size and ascends at one point to 11,400 feet. This scenic and majestic mountain comprises a sky-cresting peak, rolling foothills, lush green grass, flowery vegetation, and an elegant assortment of beautiful trees.

The pristine woods which enwrap the Sacred Mountain are unlike any others found in North America, for these silent giants are believed to be the living essence of a magical story which was sung to Apache children centuries ago. This is that story.

According to the storyteller, there was once an early phase in the beginning of the world called the Before Time. In that far-off place, there were many peoples and tribes that were given the breath of life by the creator of the world. He was known as Spirit Father, Sky Father, or the Giver of Life.

Yet even as they were created, some tribes disappeared. The reason for their departure is not fully known. What is recalled is the fact that they were people no different from you or I who lived in a world of beauty, elegance, and abundance. A hundred varieties of animal lay open to their hunting skills. The bounty of the freshwater rivers and streams were theirs to select from. From horizon to horizon, the virgin land lay beautiful, unspoiled, and undisturbed.

Above the first people of the land, the blue canopy was filled with birds and billowing clouds. Daily they flaunted their vast array of dances and put on performances which have never been duplicated. Almost as if by command, the sun would appear and give brilliance to its boundless domain. This was the world of the ancients.

The first people of the land were known by many names. Some were called the Corn People. Others were People of the Water. Still others were known as Invisible Ones, Snake House People, Valley People, Owl Clan, and a host of other names. Prominent among the first people was one tribe who would later be remembered as the Eternal Ones.

Far away from the desert which would later become their home, the Eternal Ones were little more than a clan of people living in the Northland region of the eastern mountains. Their home was situated in a very hostile climate. The frigid winds blew constantly and the snows and ice never seemed to depart. For them, the barren land was a place of bitter winters and freezing temperatures. Even the sun refused to make daily visits. As a result, the area remained bleak and isolated.

Northlanders were a hardy breed. Their bodies, like their skin and the rest of their senses, could withstand the most inclement seasons. For five generations they had carved out a meager existence from the resistant terrain. They did not have much, and what they did possess was torn from the stubborn landscape. They were a strong people. But despite their strengths and enduring capabilities, they remained an unhappy lot. Throughout the tribe, which numbered some five thousand, hardly anyone could be found who ever smiled.

The Northlanders, as they called themselves, had become as hard as the icy, rocky ground itself. Their past and their future seemed to many as somber as the snowy landscape which surrounded them. Few in the tribe believed that things would ever improve.

The seasonal return of winter had just begun to lash out at the land when the chief of the tribe called together the Council of Elders. This unusual nocturnal meeting was implemented at the behest of the tribal medicine man, Two Moons. As each elder walked from his tepee to the main lodge, he struggled with the fierce winds, which clawed at him like a vengeful winter giant. To a man, they wondered what could be so important.

The chief of the tribe was an aged warrior who had weathered some fifty snows. His name was Tall Shadow, and he was like the hard, savage land itself; he had taken the leadership away from his predecessor by personal combat. It was a tribal tradition. No one ever questioned the method, but many felt that Tall Shadow had not developed into as good a leader as he had been a warrior. Presently he ruled the clan by fear rather than loyalty. When he called for this nighttime council meeting, no one dared to be absent.

Two Moons was older than Tall Shadow. Nevertheless, as medicine man, he respected the chief's wishes. However, on this particular night, the meeting was of his own doing, not the chief's. In all the years they had sat on the council together, the two had never had much in common. Tall Shadow had no animosity towards the medicine man, but there were times when the chief wished the shaman would endorse his wishes more readily. Presently he awaited Two Moons and the council in his tepee. Outside the tent, it was cold, dark and wintry.

The flap of the chief's council lodge was a large rectangular affair. Large enough to allow an adult through, its basic function was to keep out drafts and snow flurries. One by one the elders arrived through the flap. Shaking free of the snow which had accumulated on their aged heads, they sat down in a round circle. A warm fire was located in the center of the lodge. After the arrival of the medicine man, the flap was sealed and guarded by two warriors, who sat outside the tepee in silence.

"I have called this special meeting at the request of Two Moons," the chief said, taking his place at the head of the council. "I shall allow him to tell you what he has revealed to me."

"I have had a vision," the medicine man began, opening his aged hands to the circle of elders. "I have been advised by our Sky Father that our people will soon receive a visitor. She will come from the lands to the south. It will be her task to lead us back there. Along the way, she will teach us what we need to know in order to understand the meaning of our journey. The Sky Father has also warned that if we do not heed her words, we shall burn at the whim of others."

"But this has been our home since my memory began!" complained one elder. "We must not desert our birthplace."

"We cannot move now!" another voice cautioned. "The winter has just begun and it will be months before it will yield to a season when we can travel, if we must."

"What assurance do we have that this woman will know the way or even speak our language?" remarked a third. "Traveling in this season would mean death for many adults, not to mention the children. And, if we are to be at the whim of a strange woman, we may all burn in the land to the south."

"Are you certain of that vision?" was the concern of one very influential member of the circle. With more dissenting voices increasing the growing volume, the medicine man held up his gnarled hand and the council instantly grew quiet.

"The vision was made clear to me," Two Moons assured them. "We will leave within ten days. She will arrive in five. Our path will be chosen by her and our way is clear. The Sky Father will favor those who will acknowledge his purpose and generosity. Those who will not go will die here in the icy cold. Those willing to journey will receive the gifts of the Sky Father through the woman's guidance."

"Does the Sky Father intend for us all to arrive in the Southland?" questioned one curious member of the circle. "Does he have more in store for us than just a change of location? What will be this woman's name?"

"We shall journey to the place selected for us," explained Two Moons. "Those who follow without fear will father the future. Those who question his word or fail to appreciate his gifts will remind the future of the consequences by becoming immortal. The woman's name will be Bashi."

"Immortal? What does that mean, Two Moons?" asked the chief, struck by the complexity of the prophecy. "How will Bashi make immortality a punishment? What gifts are we to receive? How will the coming of one woman change our lifestyle? What does it mean to burn at the whim of others? To date, our 'generous' Sky Father has given us nothing! We are taught nothing! That which we have has come from our own efforts."

Then the chief began to assert his multiple concerns. As was the custom, he had to be heard without interruption. Finally, when he had described the austere and most difficult life of the average tribesman, he began to remind the council that they were the descendants of the forefathers. As such, they had wrestled from the harsh environment all they called home. To abandon it all in favor of a vision would be to chance death in a strange land. "We live day to day with the miserable wind tugging at our elbows," he continued. "The morsels of food we eat are exacted from the land at a terrible price. Men die trying to rip out an existence from bitter soil. Our women's bodies have become as hard as the land they till. Our children play games not with each other, but with the shadow of death. And now we are asked to believe that a single vision, a single woman, a single journey, will give us immortality."

"Do we have a choice?" a council member asked the medicine man. "If Tall Shadow is right, we will allow our children to be buried in a far-off land which none of us have ever seen. Most of us are content. Why move? Why move at all?"

"It is the wish of our Sky Father," explained Two Moons sincerely. "The vision was given. I have presented it to you, the council. Tall Shadow now has to decide what to do. Your voice will influence his. Like the rest of our people, I must live by your combined decision."

As custom dictated, the medicine man now allowed every member of the council to speak his mind. However long or however rambling, the member's speech was heard. The last to speak was the newest and youngest member of the council. His name was White Bear. His bravery and the fact that he constantly proved it was a growing irritation to Tall Shadow. Nevertheless, even the chief had to listen to the valiant warrior.

"I am not as proficient in prophecy as my uncle, our shaman," the lad began. "However, I am not bothered by the fact that a change of climate is in our future. Personally, I welcome a place where our spears will not bounce off the game we hunt, a place where our women can turn the soil instead of snow, a place where our children are warmed by the sun, not our little fires. If this strange woman is to be our guide, I think we should allow the voice of our Sky Father to speak from any source he chooses."

The eyes of Tall Shadow never strayed from the confident council member. He felt a surge of jealousy in seeing what was a mirror image of himself thirty years ago. The young man commanded attention when he spoke, and that was beginning to worry the old chief. Tall Shadow could see the strength of White Bear. His arms and legs, like his body, were sinewy, hard, and rippling, and exhibited the promise of power. His face, although handsome and youthful, displayed the scars of several personal combats. Tall Shadow suspected that in White Bear he saw a rival, for the leadership of the tribe.

"And if she leads the tribe to disaster?" argued Tall Shadow. "It has happened before. Consider the story of the Invisible Ones. Once they lived in the mountains to the west of us. They too journeyed south. They have never been heard of since. Would you risk the lives of your people on a single dream?"

"If that dream was mine, no," replied White Bear. "But it appeared to Two Moons, and I, for one, trust his judgment."

With that wisdom-filled statement, the council was swayed to approve the vision. Despite further arguments from Tall Shadow, who nearly reversed the council's opinion, the decision was made to accept the strange woman in friendship and as an emissary of their Sky Father.

It was traditional among the Northlanders for the chief to gather together the members of the governing council and hear what they had to say concerning a particular issue. However, he was not obligated to take their advice. He could, in point of fact, take an opposite position and a different course of action. Yet it had proved difficult in the past to govern the tribe if the choice led to failure or death. Few chiefs ever remained leader long if they opposed the council's advice and then suffered a series of failures.

Tall Shadow was not so foolish as to allow failure to tarnish his reputation. On the other hand, he was not careless enough to allow any member of the council or the tribe to suggest something which might favor success. Aware that Two Moons was seldom wrong about his visions, he had to consider the possibility the shaman might be right. However, there were a few incidents which his medicine man had predicted that had not altogether proved conducive to the well-being of the people.

The following day the elders of the tribe allowed the chief to announce that a woman stranger would come and lead the tribe on a journey south. The chief emphasized that it was a vision of the medicine man that had prompted the statement.

In his announcement to the people, Tall Shadow pointed out that even though he would rather stay, as his ancestors wished, in the land of his birth, he could not change the mind of the council. As advised, he would heed the word of the Giver of Life. He therefore ordered the people to receive the woman with respect and without fear. He gave instructions that whoever found her was to bring the visitor to the main lodge near the center of the camp.

The next few days were spent in great industry. The people began assembling everything of value and preparing to transport it with them wherever they went. No one knew how long they would travel or if anyone would make it to the destination. What they did receive were suggestions from White Bear on the kinds of food they should prepare and what provisions were necessary. It wasn't long before the five days were spent; the tribe awoke on the sixth morning and awaited the arrival of the visitor.

Some of the people waited on the major paths to the village. All expected to be the first to see her. Others waited on the trails leading down from the mountain. But the great majority was certain she would arise from the waters in the river next to the camp. It had happened before. What none of the people expected was for her to be already in the camp.

The councilmen of the tribe, dressed in their finest array, were busy preparing a welcome in the main lodge. The chief was waiting in his tepee for any member of his flanking scouts to bring him news of the woman's arrival. White Bear was not sure where she might appear from, so he decided to wait in the main assembly area directly in the center of the camp. There, with a few other warriors, he paced up and down in the drizzling mist, attempting to stay warm and also trying to keep the ceremonial gifts from becoming soaked.

It was not White Bear's habit to be taken unaware. In fact, he prided himself in always being alert to his surroundings and aware of anyone who happened to come near him. With his strong hands he shifted the various heavy coverings from one object to another, shielding as many gifts as he could with the limited sizes available.

The gifts were not rare or expensive, as per the instructions of Tall Shadow. The chief didn't wish to give the impression to strangers of his tribe being a wealthy one. He considered such display unnecessary. True emissaries from the Giver of Life, the chief explained, would already be wealthy. Therefore, all tribal valuables were to remain in his keeping.

Examining the poor gifts and small offerings, White Bear was embarrassed by the limited expression of the tribe's welcome. It was true his people as a whole were not wealthy in any sense of the word, but he, like the rest of his people, was aware that the tribe did possess gifts of real value.

White Bear, for instance, wore his finest hand-stitched garments made of rare white fox, which was lined and fringed with black bear fur. On his wrists he sported silver bracelets, awards for courage. Around his neck he displayed the exquisitely sculptured ivory medallion his parents had given him before they died. The necklace contained inlaid silver and was encrusted with semiprecious stones and rare Kodiak bear claws. All in all, it was a beautiful and priceless possession.

After studying the inadequate gifts awhile, White Bear looked about. Seeing that no one was anywhere near him, he took out his precious family heirloom and placed it on the small pile of gifts. No sooner had he completed his gesture of personal offering when he suddenly felt the presence of someone directly behind him. He heard a soft, gentle, feminine voice whisper, "Your gift is accepted and appreciated."

Instinct, agility, and blinding speed allowed White Bear to pivot on one foot, snatch a war club with his right hand and a shield with his left, and spin away to defend himself against the unexpected assailant. All his training and personal experience had taught him that a warrior who struck first would usually prevail in a fight to the death.

Holding the war axe high over his head, White Bear froze and discovered that his target was a woman. Despite the possibility of instant death from the weapon poised above her, she made no attempt to protect herself. Instead she stood politely, looking up at him with her glistening, coal-black eyes. White Bear knew immediately she was not one of his people. He had never seen her before. For one thing, her dress was plain and simple and did not compare with the colorful Ndee finery of the day.

"If you kill me," she whispered slowly and without alarm, "my journey will have been wasted."

"Who are you?" questioned White Bear, still holding his axe above his head.

"My name is Bashi B'as'hil. Spirit Woman. I will be your guide."

White Bear stood as motionless as a statue, wearing a profound look of genuine surprise on his wet face. While he stood in quiet astonishment, word of the stranger's magical appearance spread across the camp like brushfire. In no time at all, the chief was told, the council informed, and the tribe assembled. It was the first time in White Bear's memory that his people had ever responded so quickly to anything. Slowly recovering his composure, White Bear suggested to the crowd that they should stand near the circle until the council and the chief arrived.

While the murmuring tribe shifted about the circle boundary which marked the tribal assembly area, White Bear studied the astonishing woman. She was not old enough to be a matron; on the other hand, she was past the youth of a maid. White Bear estimated her age at twenty, and concluded that wherever she came from, she was a generous sight, even in her simple and plain attire. Her natural physical gifts were ample.

When the chief arrived with the council in tow, a hush fell over the people. Everyone was staring at how plainly the young woman was dressed. They had been told to wear their finest costumes to meet someone of an extraordinary nature, yet most of the muttering concerned how shabbily their visitor was dressed.

The chief and the council cared little how the stranger was dressed. Asking the tribe for quiet, Tall Shadow motioned for the woman to speak. Standing to one side, White Bear noticed something. The air was misty cold, the breeze miserable, and the ground like ice. Yet without showing the least discomfort, the woman turned leisurely to face the people. Few even noticed that she was barefooted.

"The journey will begin now," Bashi explained. "I will be your guide. The Great Father will provide for you as he has done all these years."

"How far is this land you will take us to?" questioned Tall Shadow, addressing Bashi as she stood before the council. "How long will it take? What promise of immortality do you bring to us? Tell us about this warning that Two Moons spoke of. 'If we fail to learn the lessons of life, we will burn at the request of others?' What does that mean?"

"The land the Great Father has selected for you is a far journey from here. It is warm and the sun will fill all the days of your lives. You will behold natural wonders of unparalleled beauty. Your children will want for little.

In the spring and summer you will hunt. In the fall you will receive the abundance of Earth Mother and give thanks to her and Sky Father in your songs, chants, and prayers."

While Bashi spoke of the wonders that would fill the future days of the people, Tall Shadow tried to construct a means by which these gifts would be seen as his doing. Such wealth and wonders as Bashi described could earn him rewards untold as well as the admiration and gratitude of everyone. Perhaps then he could expect a great deal more of his position.

Not everyone's head was filled with visions of grandeur and untold riches. Two Moons caught White Bear looking in his direction. Each was troubled with the possibility of sudden wealth. They were certain the promise of their new home carried with it a price the tribe would be unprepared for. No one had ever thanked Sky Father or Earth Mother for anything; in the people's estimation, neither had offered them anything. What they possessed was not given, the people said, but torn away from the clutches of Sky Father and Earth Mother. Yet as Bashi went on, Two Moons and White Bear each felt a ray of hope that the people could in fact learn to give thanks.

Most people in the tribe were skeptical that such a place as Bashi described existed. They hoped that Tall Shadow would require Bashi to specify where this new home would be. They wanted proof, not promises.

"The words of your Sky Father have been written in my heart," revealed Bashi, walking about in the mist. "You have been given much and are now promised more. Those of you who heed my words now will come to be feared by all. Embrace the land that Sky Father gives you, though it be dry and empty, and you will be strong. Endure the land, though it be forsaken, and you will not want for pride. Unite with the land, though it be hostile, and it will become your ally. But forget to thank the spirits, and you will pray for all eternity."

"Are these the words of the Sky Father?" Tall Shadow asked with some dryness in his throat. "They say nothing of burning at the whims of others."

"Those who forget to honor the spirits," finished Bashi, staring directly into the chief's eyes, "those who cannot raise their hands and voices to the sky and give thanks for all they have received will be subject to that portion of his promise."

The overcast sky was still drizzling with a fine mist when the chief offered Bashi a seat near the council in the great lodge. During the meal, she was shown her gifts; only Tall Shadow was surprised when the necklace belonging to White Bear was presented. The gift brought a wide smile to Bashi's face and even the council was impressed. They knew how much the gift meant to White Bear.

The chief was not a man who would break with tradition. Even though the gifts were offered on behalf of the entire tribe, he knew everyone would realize the necklace was given by White Bear. As chief, he could not allow a junior member of his tribe to offer a superior gift to a visitor. He would have to give one of greater value.

Though it caused him much inner turmoil, he nevertheless sent for his store of gifts, and, in an unprecedented move, gave them to Bashi. This caused a great murmuring in the tribe. They had never seen Tall Shadow behave so generously and wondered what it meant.

White Bear and Two Moons saw that although Bashi accepted the gifts, she did not smile as broadly as at the single one given by White Bear. This incensed Tall Shadow. Still, he kept his composure and said nothing. This, too, was in keeping with tradition.

In the days to come, Tall Shadow gave White Bear so many tasks to complete, that he was kept away from Bashi for the next several days. White Bear was sent to the far reaches of the tribal territory to retrieve whatever food could be had from the many traps and snares of the tribe. In addition, he was given the task of ensuring that all families were listed and prepared for the journey.

The morning the long journey began was the first of many days the Northlanders would remember well. The wind had stopped blowing, the constantly black sky now turned a modest gray, and the distant horizon was seen for the first time in their memory. Everyone was anxious to begin; this included the children who, more than their elders, swarmed around Bashi playfully.

With everyone intent on crowding around her, Bashi used her powers to help motivate them to travel. The children who surrounded the beautiful guide were sure they had her encircled. Yet when Tall Shadow tried to reach her through the throng, Bashi was found to have disappeared. A runner informed the people she was far ahead, which forced everyone to gather their belongings and follow her.

What was planned as a month's travel resulted in a longer journey than anyone had ever dreamed possible. The chief and the elders were hard-pressed to keep pace with their scouts, who swore that Bashi was just ahead of them. Yet time after time, when anyone tried to reach her, she was found to be farther ahead than expected.

Several months of hard traveling later, the tribe came to rest near a dry river bed. The children were exhausted and crying loudly, the women complained that there was no water, and the men, despite their best efforts, found no game to hunt.

Within the great tepee, the council met and asked Tall Shadow what he proposed to do about the mounting problems. Unable to answer, Tall Shadow promised he would find solutions. Away from the ears of the council and the prying eyes of his people, Tall Shadow ordered White Bear to explain why Bashi had abandoned them in a wasteland. After all, it was White Bear who trusted her, not he. Accepting the blame, White Bear promised to find Bashi and ask her. Unfortunately, like everyone else, he had no idea where she had disappeared to.

On the hill overlooking the dry river, White Bear sat and wondered what had become of the enchanting Bashi. Then, just as she had done many times before, she appeared directly behind him. Instinctively, White Bear knew it was her. Her ability to come and go at will impressed White Bear. Since it had become her habit to do this, he did not react. Instead he continued to stare far ahead and, when he felt her approach, remained seated on a large rock he had discovered.

"Our food supply is exhausted, as are the children," White Bear explained without turning to face Bashi. "The women have no water and the men are tired of chasing the empty horizon. Where are the gifts of Earth Mother you promised?"

"You need to learn the secrets of Earth Mother," Bashi whispered, putting a hand to White Bear's shoulder. "The gifts will come from knowledge and skill. Sky Father will allow you to drink when you are thirsty. He will feed you when you are hungry. You may rest here, or follow me tomorrow, and in four weeks time you will have all these things."

Unsure if it was his doubt or her certainty that convinced him, White Bear stood up, at the same time reaching for her hand. A look of profound surprise flushed over White Bear as he turned and instead of Bashi found Two Moons. When White Bear touched his hand, Two Moons suddenly awoke from a trance and asked White Bear the reason he had been summoned.

Unable to explain why he had summoned the medicine man to his side, White Bear asked the old man if he knew the whereabouts of Bashi. The medicine man too was visibly confused as to what had become of her. The last thing he remembered was chanting with her in his tepee. The next thing Two Moons remembered, he was standing next to White Bear on the bluff overlooking the dry river bed.

There were times in White Bear's life when he was confused. It wasn't often, but when he was, it was distressing. Lately it occurred whenever Bashi appeared.

At such times things happened which caused his mind to whirl. Her voice was one such phenomenon. It was unmistakable, and yet it had emanated from the body of Two Moons, who also couldn't explain it. Her presence always produced a feeling of quiet serenity. Yet a dozen times, when White Bear thought he was talking to her, he discovered it was someone else.

Nevertheless, he was certain of the value of her advice and direction. In the months since the journey had begun, Bashi kept the entire caravan moving southward, always southward. Days and weeks passed with the tribe's list of complaints growing steadily. White Bear was sure the information given by the spirit of Bashi was guaranteed to alleviate their pain.

Concluding that the information was factual, White Bear related to Tall Shadow, word for word, what Bashi had promised. Empowered with this information, Tall Shadow gathered and assured the people that all would be well. He gave them his word. In four weeks time, he promised, they would arrive.

Much grumbling and dissatisfaction followed, but since their chief seemed sincere in his word, the people held silent on their complaints. They had no way of knowing, but this would be the first time the entire tribe would go so long without food or water.

They forced themselves to travel hundreds upon hundreds of miles. Day after day they followed their guide, who never seemed to tire, yet always appeared ahead, entreating them to follow.

The four weeks passed quickly and the Northlanders covered so much territory they no longer felt as if they were a part of the icy country. The tribe realized they were in a different part of the world altogether. They did not recognize the colorful landscape. The area was not bleak, cold, or frozen, as their homeland had been. Neither was the living panorama which they viewed with hungry eyes barren and lifeless. They were not subject to the bitter winds, or the biting rains. The land they traversed now was a welcome change indeed.

In addition to the new territory other changes were apparent. Their bodies, which had survived the rigors of the journey, had also undergone a dramatic transformation. They had become accustomed to the torturous physical demands imposed on them. Adults and children alike had had their inner resolve developed, honed, and tempered on a thousand mile anvil. Their spirits had hardened, their determination fixed. They were a new tribe of people altogether.

The dawning sun of the fourth week produced a magnificent sunrise and as it arched high over them, the sky burst open and revealed the deepest tint of blue they had ever seen. The children marveled at the great spirals of billowing white clouds above them, while below their feet the warm sands surged up and filled their hearts with contentment.

Despite being hungry and thirsty, the entire tribe basked in the radiant warmth of the bright yellow sun. The people filled their lungs with the abundant fresh air and felt truly alive. Many began wearing wide smiles of happiness. As they looked behind them, they could see where they had been. Now they looked ahead and saw clearly for the first time that they were standing on virgin ground. It was a dark, rich land which held the black roots of endless miles of green grass. In every direction they turned, they beheld countless natural wonders.

The majority of the tribe didn't realize that what they were viewing was the wide, expansive earth in the light of the sun. Nevertheless, it helped them to distinguish the mountain range they had somehow scaled. Everything they saw below was majestically sculptured. On this dawn of the fourth week, the chief stood on a high promontory overlooking the vast plain. Calling everyone's attention to it, he pointed across the open expanse to show that he had kept his word.

The Northlanders had never beheld such breathtaking beauty in their entire lives. Young and old stood wide-eyed, open-mouthed and awestruck as they viewed the boundless horizon carpeted with miles of billowing prairie grass. They marveled at how it swayed like an ocean of green waves. In the distance they saw numerous herds of deer and antelope running freely. Great flocks of birds of all species took flight at their approach.

While the chief took credit for bringing them to such a wondrous land, he arranged for White Bear, and anyone else who might dispute his boast, to be out hunting. His orders were explicit. The hunters were not to return until they had completely replenished the tribe's exhausted stock. Meanwhile, Tall Shadow established camp near the glittering, winding river his hunters had located earlier.

In the next several days, a great celebration was planned. Meanwhile, another tribe, just as exhausted and thirsty as the Ndee clan had been when they had first arrived, was discovered passing through the territory. In the spirit of good will, White Bear suggested the Northlanders share their discoveries and invite the strangers to feast with them.

The idea of sharing what the tribe had laid claim to was shouted down angrily by Tall Shadow. He was supported by the majority of the people. They, like him, refused to give away what was rightfully theirs. Moreover, Tall Shadow decided the passing tribe must be destroyed before they camped along his river. He was of the opinion that the Northlanders had discovered the mountain and all its bounty, and they should have no intentions, now or ever, of sharing any of it.

War was close behind Tall Shadow and his followers. Despite opposition from White Bear and a small portion of the tribe, they could not dissuade the selfish chief. He had discovered the place and was determined to keep it. In short order, the passing tribe was engaged and decimated. Tall Shadow returned in triumph and proclaimed the mountaintop feast would be held to celebrate his victory instead of to praise the spirits.

Two Moons and White Bear pleaded with him to remember that they had been given everything they possessed. Now they were in a new land, but it would never be truly theirs if they made war on everyone who wandered through. White Bear reminded the people that the celebration should be held in honor of Sky Father and Earth Mother for all they had given.

Despite the fervent arguments of White Bear and Two Moons, the Northlanders and their chief were not convinced. Barely a handful of followers, numbering some two hundred out of some two thousand, refused to participate in the celebration. The feast was well into its fullness when Bashi made an unexpected appearance before the unruly followers of Tall Shadow.

Against the backdrop of thunderous drums, raucous laughter, and loud celebration, Bashi spoke to all ears that paused to listen. She informed Tall Shadow that the land which he had taken in blood was meant to be shared by all the children of the Giver of Life. It was sacred. Now, because it was stained, it would forever yield only bitter memories for their children.

The summit upon which they stood was reserved for contemplation, prayer, and reverence. It was not to be used in praise of death. Bashi fervently reminded the people that their home in the new land had been established with only one covenant. They were to receive the gifts of Earth Mother and Sky Father, but only if they raised their arms in thankful prayer and grateful song.

At this point, Tall Shadow and his followers became angry and riotous, challenging the promise of "gifts" made by Bashi. Where, they demanded, were the gifts? They had not seen anything given to them. Everything they had possessed before in the Northland and everything they now claimed and held sovereignty over was theirs by discovery. They had endured much and were certain they had earned whatever they now possessed.

This outburst caused Bashi to raise her hand and remind Tall Shadow in a threatening voice that the bestowing of gifts had begun long ago in the Northland.

Further, the journey had been strewn with rigors so that the mettle of the people could be tested. The harsh Northland seasons had made them nearly invulnerable to hostile climates. The dark environment had given them the ability to see in poor light. Their hard skin was shelter against any storm. Truly these gifts were priceless.

Despite the truth of Bashi's words, Tall Shadow convinced the people that, regardless of the gifts, they were still children of the Giver of Life and he owed much to them. This was too much for White Bear, who arose and accused his people of being selfish and ungrateful. What more was expected of Sky Father? If a parent gave a child a gift which benefited the child, should not the child raise his voice and arms in gratitude? This outburst only caused the people to split between the chief and White Bear. Loud arguments erupted.

To be grateful to anyone was not in the nature of Northlanders, shouted many. It promoted weakness and cowardice. This point was echoed by Tall Shadow. What they had now they owed to themselves and not to any parent. He asked if any of his followers wanted to raise their arms in prayer or thanks for being on the mountain. No one replied. Again he asked if they wanted to sing praises to Earth Mother for anything they had seen or enjoyed. His question was not answered.

With silence the only reply, Bashi warned Tall Shadow that whoever refused would regret it for all eternity. If they would not raise their arms now, they would have to do so the rest of their lives. White Bear urged the people to change their stubborn attitudes. Two Moons added his voice and reminded them of the curse of immortality. This drew taunting defiance. The more brazen shouted that they dreamed of becoming immortal.

Failing to convince the supporters of Tall Shadow, Bashi led White Bear and his small group of followers down the rock-and grass-encrusted mountain. Loud jeers, laughter, and name-calling followed them. The night was clear, the temperature warm. Yet by the time the small band had reached the bottom of the treeless mountain, the breeze had chilled dramatically.

Bashi praised Two Moons and White Bear for the valiant effort they exhibited. She could not emphasize enough the importance of praising Sky Father and Earth Mother. She promised that they would become the leaders of their people. They had earned the gifts of the land and all of nature's prizes for they understood the importance of sharing and giving thanks.

Before leaving, Bashi instructed everyone to ignore the sounds of merriment on the mountain or any other sounds which might be heard later that night. Above all, no one was to return to the mountain summit. They were instructed to wait for four days and then to celebrate their new home with a dance and prayer to Sky Father and Earth Mother. Bashi asked that they do so barefoot, so that they would be in contact with their mother the earth.

The people did as they were told. They ignored the sounds of revelry spilling down from the mountain. These loud and cheerful festival sounds were soon overpowered by an unbelievable display of lightning, thunder, and violent trembling. The entire mountain endured several massive quakes before becoming still and silent.

Four days after the mountain shook and churned with its display of brilliant, luminous lights and rumbling thunder, Two Moons and White Bear led their people in a spirited festival of singing and merriment, including dances and chants of praise to Bashi, the wandering spirit. They proclaimed loudly their appreciation to Sky Father and Earth Mother for all the wonders of the land. The dancing concluded with the grateful people raising their arms up into the sky.

Several weeks passed and Two Moons wondered why the followers of Tall Shadow had not come down from the mountain. Time should have allowed them to realize the error of their ways, yet no one appeared. White Bear decided to send word that his men had enjoyed a successful hunt and would be honored if Tall Shadow and his people would join them in a feast.

Several messengers were dispatched up the mountain, but they returned much later saying that there was no sign of Tall Shadow or his followers. They also reported that where there had been no woods before on the great mountain, there was now no section of its surface without them.

This surprising revelation caused Two Moons and White Bear to ascend to the summit and discover for themselves what had happened to their former friends. When they arrived, the report given by their messengers was confirmed. The landscape, which before had been a rocky and treeless mound, was now a beautiful combination of evergreens and pine woods. As far as the eye could see there were trees.

This presented a mystery to White Bear and Two Moons, who, with several groups of hunters, searched and searched for hours. They found no trace of any of their wayward people. When at last they concluded that every one had somehow vanished, White Bear sent the men home. Later, as he and Two Moons were walking down from the summit, they unexpectedly heard low moaning.

Searching for the location of so pitiful a sound, they continued until they were convinced that the moans were in fact originating from inside the large trees. They were about to examine them in closer detail when Bashi suddenly appeared at their side.

"The source of the moaning you hear is the languishing prayer of your companions and former tribe members," assured Bashi, leading them to the tallest of the pine trees. "They would not lift their arms to pray and give thanks before, so now they will do so for all eternity. Passersby will think it is only the wind blowing through the trees."

As the trio approached the largest of the great trees, they saw how it arose from the ground and shot several hundred feet into the air. They marveled at its massive roots, which sank deep into the black soil, then lunged upwards into the thick frame of a trunk and culminated in the twisted arms of its gnarled branches. These lofty appendages gave the impression of uplifted arms held stationary in permanent prayer.

When at last they examined the bark of the tree, they saw an image which resembled a human face. From within the tree itself, the saddest, deepest moan could be heard. Stepping away in alarm, both men looked at Bashi, who smiled and then disappeared. As the smoke evaporated, they heard her whisper, "They would not lift their arms in prayer; now they will do so for all eternity. They craved immortality, so forever they will be known as the Immortal Ones."[4]

---

4   The prophecy of Bashi, who warned that the immortals would burn at the whims of others, comes true each time you hear someone suggest, "Throw another log into the fire." The immortals cannot die, but can be released to join the spirits.

The Legend of the Mountain Mystic

The spirits of earth, fire, wind, and water figure prominently in the Apache creation story. In this magical womb of the spirit realm exist the guardians of spirit people whom the Apache call the "Ancients." It is they, the Apache believe, who add reality to a world filled with wonders. Primary among these spirits are Daughter Without Eyes, Sun Boy, Corn Woman, Ghost Spider, and Dream Maker. Others such as Vulture and Crayfish come second to man, but one ghostly voice is not. He is known as the Mountain Mystic, D'zit'diy'ini. This is his story.

Long ago, in a desert near the Sacred Mountain, there lived a nomadic clan whom their descendants would call Sand People. They were a small tribe barely one hundred in number. Yet, for all practical purposes, they possessed sufficient forces for their needs. They were primarily hunters and gatherers. Occasionally they attempted sedentary ways of life which included pottery making, basket weaving, and dry farming.

It was not unusual for these people to succeed in any number of these projects. From time to time they even excelled in their minor efforts and managed to stock sufficient stores with which to trade. When they did trade, they traded for what they lacked. Among these items were rare animal pelts. This occasional trade led to a tribal desire to obtain rarities.

Though the best of weapons were produced, traded for, or secured, the hunters lacked the skill to use them. Try as they might, they spent a great deal of time learning and refining the habits of the most elusive quarries only to realize their efforts were woefully inadequate. Moreover, those who taught them, the forest and woods instructors, lacked the insight to obtain the elusive secrets of the forests and deserts.

Thus it remained for generations; hunters and trappers alike were born, aged, and died. Yet the best of them, however long they lived, gained only a modest reputation for knowing the secrets of the animals. Even the most notable were only moderately successful. This is how it stayed, moderately successful. The hunters, ambitious and eager to a fault, desperately awaited a leader who would be able to teach them the inner habits of every woodland creature.

That individual appeared in the year of the Dark Wind. He was born to a family already composed of several other children. The mother, an industrious woman of middle age, was called Running Deer. Her manner was understanding and caring. The father, an aging warrior named Fallen Oak, was, despite his years, able to hold his own against assailants of other tribes. He was a man of skill and courage and was well respected.

The children of Fallen Oak and Running Deer had grown fast and obtained the basic skills of life taught them by their family and elders. None disappointed their teachers. The boys, numbering three in all, became adept at running, fighting, and helping their father with his meager hunting trophies.

The girls, both of them, had with little effort developed as proficient in their duties as any in the tribe. They were skilled enough to become wives and were marked for marriage when they reached maturity. All in all, they were a typical and normal family.

The family had no way of knowing that the youngest son was anything but normal. For the first ten years of his life, things went about without any indication of strangeness. However, when he reached the age of eleven, Running Deer saw a definite change in her son. The observation was also noted by the watchful eyes of his father.

Fallen Oak and his wife had named their youngest son after a melodic wind which coincided with a golden moon they saw in the sky during their youthful courtship. The boy was called Moon Song, and they loved him dearly. Running Deer felt a great loneliness in him. Fallen Oak saw him display normal physical skills, but he, too, felt Moon Song was different.

The differences observed by his parents were soon evident to those who came in contact with Moon Song. In the beginning, his brothers always included him in their games. They helped him understand the sometimes difficult lessons taught to him by instructors.

Moon Song was often asked by his sisters to help with special chores which called for a group effort. They enjoyed his company. Like other boys his age, he was invited to accompany hunting parties on short excursions. Tribal boys found his presence unobtrusive and friendly. Moon Song was always excited when asked to join any activity. He especially enjoyed learning about the world around him and was ceaselessly asking questions.

Then one day things began to change. The invitations dwindled and eventually ceased altogether. His brothers, sisters, friends, and elders all found excuses for not asking Moon Song along. It wasn't readily known by his parents why others were beginning to shun and ignore him. No one spoke of it, and the boy was too discouraged to discuss it with his father.

Fallen Oak and Running Deer remained ignorant of the fact that their son was being excluded from social interaction. Then one day, they saw it for themselves. A group of boys were gaming in physical combat at which Moon Song had proven to be a good sport. His father noticed that the boys were short one player and sent his son over to them. However, as Moon Song approached, the boys all decided they had chores to finish.

Fallen Oak accepted this without comment until the act repeated itself several times. Things finally came to a head when Running Deer saw her daughters having a very difficult time with a task and asked Moon Song to help them. The sisters balked, claiming they could do it without his help.

After this incident, and after compiling similar stories from friends and neighbors, the parents called for a family council. Sending Moon Song to an uncle, on the pretense that the elder needed help with a chore, the family discussed the problem. Beginning with the eldest son, Fallen Oak and Running Deer began hearing such unbelievable stories that they insisted that all their children swear they were telling the truth.

The tales Fallen Oak and Running Deer heard were incredible. So much so, they decided to check with neighbors and friends. Their stories confirmed the fact that Moon Song could often be found standing alone and talking to the wind. Stranger still was the observation that Moon Song was easily distracted by animals. Word had it that Moon Song would stop whatever he was doing and converse with them. It was eerie.

If one continued to observe the boy, one could see that regardless of the kind of animal, Moon Song was apparently on friendly terms with it. In the beginning, his actions produced only laughs, jeers, and jokes. But then later, the mirth stopped, and a more serious note replaced it. Anyone seen with Moon Song was thought as unbalanced as he.

This, then, was the fantastic problem that Fallen Oak and Running Deer had to deal with. They were hard-pressed to see anything but trouble in his actions. They decided that, for the time being, the boy had better be cajoled into having fewer interactions with the animals. This was what Running Deer suggested. For her son's own good, the boy was offered other outlets for his odd pursuits.

On the advice of an elder, Fallen Oak took his son on a trip into the mountains. Along the way they talked. Moon Song was asked if there was anything he wanted to discuss. At first, the boy pretended ignorance as if he did not know what his father was talking about. Fallen Oak did his best to avoid prying into his son's problems. It was not only courtesy, but tradition. He waited for several days and then tried again.

As sunset allowed the night curtain to descend, on the fifth day of their journey, a mountain lion was heard prowling near their camp. Having dealt with lions before, Fallen Oak took up his shield, spear, and adjusted his knife, telling his son to crouch low and to stay near the fire for protection. Moon Song followed his father's instructions just as the large cat made its entrance.

The mountain lion's face, and the length of his teeth, indicated a full grown adult. Its eyes promised death. With his shield up, and his long lance poised to defend, Fallen Oak felt the fear that always accompanies such a contest. He was sure he would kill the beast, but was also sure it would not be easy. Drawing nearer, the immense cat sensed Fallen Oak's fear and anticipated victory. The stalking cat drew closer still, and was on the verge of attacking, when Moon Song stood up and began singing.

The hissing and snarling of the mountain lion, and the deep breathing of his father froze in silent vapor as the melodic voice of Moon Song filled the night air. The cat's ears perked and twitched as if bothered by a pesky fly, while the eyes of Fallen Oak widened to their limits. Moon Song continued to sing. His voice was rich and clear. Holding one hand up into the night sky, he extended the other out to the poised mountain lion.

Passing his father, Moon Song touched him and motioned for him to lower his spear. Unaware of why he complied, Fallen Oak let his defensive posture melt. Stunned, he watched as his son sang directly into the face of the huge mountain cat. The great beast not only did not hiss or snarl, but allowed the boy to stroke its head several times.

With the song fading softly into the woods, the cat relaxed, walked away, then turned, and with a final loud snarl aimed towards Fallen Oak, disappeared into the darkness. Fallen Oak remained speechless for several minutes while his son sat down as if nothing had occurred. Fallen Oak did not say a word for a long while. At this point, all he could do was marvel at the power of his son to reduce a ferocious animal to a purring kitten.

Unable to restrain his curiosity any longer, Fallen Oak began asking questions. "How did you do that?" he asked admiringly.

"His spirit was angry, father," replied Moon Song innocently. "I felt his heart heavy for the loss of his mate. The cat believed we were responsible. I allowed him to read my heart and learn it was not I. Then I told him that you were my father and that you would not do such a thing."

"Did he believe you?: Fallen Oak inquired.

"It was difficult to convince him while you continued to hold your spear, father," informed Moon Song. "But once he saw that you were only trying to protect me, he knew you were not to blame either."

"How long have you been able to, uh, sing to mountain lions?" asked his father, finding it incredible.

"Since the time my eldest brother caught a beaver in his snare and I let it go," confessed Moon Song. "That night I heard the wind tell me that I was destined to learn the voices of the animals. I found it amusing at first, but then it became a curse. I was spending more time with the animals than with my friends and family. Now everyone thinks I am mad. How could I know such a gift would separate me from my family. Even you and mother feel the need to lie to me."

It was not easy for Fallen Oak to apologize for his behavior, but he did. Now he realized what everyone was so frightened of and set out to learn the full extent of his son's power. Moon Song was pleased his father saw his gift as a good omen. For the first time since he acquired his gift for communicating with animals, Moon Song felt proud.

With a magic which Fallen Oak found disturbing, Moon Song walked through the forest and sang for all the creatures to follow at his command. The animals crowded around and approached without fear. From a distance, Fallen Oak watched in awe as creature after creature appeared from the woods, and without apprehension, walked up and touched his son.

It wasn't until Moon Song showed his father that he spoke most easily with the eagle, the hawk, and the sparrow, that his father began to see potential in his son's powers. Fallen Oak observed with fascination how easy it was for Moon Song to call on the beaver, the fish, and even the bear and otter. There seemed no limit to his son's influence.

Several days later, Moon Song and his father found themselves out on a desert prairie. There, the young boy called and soon received the attention of a herd of buffalo. Fallen Oak was completely astonished and suddenly he saw how his son's gift could be of benefit to the entire tribe.

Upon returning to the camp, Fallen Oak asked for and received a special audience with the medicine man. The old shaman was not in the habit of breaking with traditional procedures for which tribal members visited him and how they approached. Except for the chief and council of elders, all others offered a gift and waited to receive an audience. The gift was to appease the spirits when asking their advice. The medicine man ate with the spirits and was allowed to accept gifts in their name.

Fallen Oak offered an armload of pelts to the medicine man's wife with the unusual request that he be allowed in immediately. The woman took the furs, and with a look of disdain for people who did not honor tradition, disappeared into the tepee. Almost instantly, she returned and signaled for Fallen Oak to enter. The shaman sat in the back of the lodge and indicated that the excited warrior should sit down.

Fallen Oak did not speak, as that would dishonor him and break further with tradition. Instead he held his silence. The shaman, whose name was Spirit Feather, deduced his old friend was anxious to relate something of importance because he was quite aware that Fallen Oak knew the proper procedure for asking for an audience with the spirits.

"Your son's powers trouble you?" asked Spirit Feather, stoking the small fire between them.

"You know of Moon Song's powers?" asked Fallen Oak, aware that very little happened to anyone in the village without the medicine man knowing something of it. "I am here to let you know that what he has shown me can be of great benefit to our people. It was foretold."

"There is a price you and your son will pay if you do as you are contemplating," warned Spirit Feather seriously. "The spirits have granted your son the power to touch their lives. He has been empowered by the Giver of Life to learn the names of all the animals. He can talk with the wind and the rain. His memory is without equal. He can command any living creature to do his bidding."

"That is what I want to bring to the attention of the council," interrupted Fallen Oak. "We have been promised that a hunter would be born to teach us the most hidden secrets of the animal world. Now we can acquire the knowledge of the wood animals and be able to hunt more successfully. Our families will not go hungry anymore."

"I can promise you, he will be successful in learning their secrets, my friend," assured Spirit Feather reluctantly. "But heed the warning of the wind and spirits. On the day an animal's life is given without good cause, the mystic voice will be silenced forever. He who would speak as a brother to all creatures will, if he betrays them, never be able to recognize any who approach him. He will live apart even from his own kind."

"My son will be true to the animals," assured Fallen Oak with a great smile. "I will see to it that he keeps his promise to them." Seeing that Fallen Oak was not taking him sufficiently seriously, Spirit Feather tried again to make his friend understand the price of his son's power. Regardless of his efforts, Fallen Oak felt the danger was of little importance.

Calling a general assembly of the great council and the tribe at large, Fallen Oak promised to reward their patience. Everyone was curious as to the reason why they were summoned. With his wife and family sitting along the rim of the great circle with other tribal members, Fallen Oak asked permission from the chief and the council to speak.

"I have great news for everyone!" announced Fallen Oak with brimming enthusiasm. "For generations we have awaited a hunter to be born unto us with the power to learn the secrets of the animal world."

"That hunter has been foreseen by our medicine man," reminded the chief. "Are you saying you know him?"

"He is a hunter who needs no weapon," began Fallen Oak walking about to ensure that everyone was able to hear him. "It is said he will learn the inner secrets of every creature. He will be able to teach all of our hunters where they may find the lairs and homes of every animal we hunt."

"Such a man would be honored by all," added an elder of the council. "You know such a warrior?"

"That warrior is my son, Moon Song!" informed Fallen Oak proudly as he reached the area where his son was sitting. "Here is the hunter whom we've all been waiting for."

Though he expected cheers and words of praise, laughter and raucous noise was his only return. It infuriated and frustrated Fallen Oak. Try as he might, he could not get the tribe to be quiet. The sea of laughing voices with their name calling, and their jeers, rained down on Moon

Song who stood silent at his father's side. He could see the disbelief in the laughing faces of his people.

His father standing dumbfounded at his people's belittling attitude, Moon Song felt that little could be said which would convince the skeptical crowd. They were sure this was some kind of practical joke. Looking into the laughing faces of his people and the disbelieving stare worn by the chief and the council, Moon Song knew a demonstration was in order.

At first, the singing of Moon Song was too soft to be heard by everyone. This was due to the volume of taunting laughter. But, as if a magical hand had passed over his people, one by one they were able to hear the soft, melodious beauty of his tune. In less time than it would have taken for the chief to gain quiet, the crowd fell silent. Every ear of every man, woman, and child in the village now listened to the depth and feeling with which the son of Fallen Oak was chanting.

The chief stood up, but not to gain quiet. Instead, he arose to see if indeed the wondrous voice was originating from the handsome youth. Approaching the singing boy, he, like everyone else, was enchanted by the melody. His heart felt free and strangely attracted to its magical sound. Then, as he came within a few yards of the boy and his father, the chief beheld something he and the tribe would never forget.

From directly overhead, in the clear blue skies above the gathering, a single, shrill voice was heard. It was the cry of an eagle. The lone majestic bird flew in wide circles as if trying to ascertain the location and origin of its caller. When it was sure, it descended without effort in narrowing circles, and landed on the extended arm of Fallen Oak.

Knowing instinctively what he should do, Fallen Oak brought the great bird down near his son. The crowd murmured loudly in awe and marveled when the eagle lowered its head to receive several strokes from the hand of Moon Song. The boy motioned for his father to move the eagle close to the chief. Somewhat unsure of his role, the chief touched the eagle and then saw Moon Song point up into the sky.

Gracefully, the eagle shot upwards into the blue ceiling and disappeared. The crowd held their silence as Moon Song began to sing yet again. This time a timber wolf appeared seemingly from out of nowhere to stand before Moon Song. The tribe held its breath as the wondrous scene concluded with Moon Song singing into the wolf's ear. Magically, the wolf licked Moon Song's hand and then turned and ran off to fade into the desert landscape.

There was no limit to the praise Fallen Oak received when Moon Song sat down with the council. The chief and all the elders were unsure how to proceed with the magical gift of the enchanted boy. The crowd eventually dispersed, with many tribal members reminding their friends and families that they knew all along Moon Song was special. Other voices claimed to be relatives or close associates of his immediate family. They chided their friends for having laughed at the young mystic.

It was decided by the council that Moon Song would begin teaching the hunters where and how the animals in the woods could be hunted, trapped, and snared. Although reluctant to betray his friends, Spirit Feather reminded Moon Song his gift had been promised by the Giver of Life. He assured him he had been born with that special destiny in mind. Then, to make everyone aware of the penalty for misusing the gift, Spirit Feather repeated the rule governing the gift to the boy and the council.

Although the rule was emphasized with great conviction, Spirit Feather observed the indifference of all who heard it. The warning was not taken seriously. He realized all the members were only interested in taking advantage of the power which had finally materialized. If there was anyone concerned with the warning, it was Moon Song.

During the ensuing weeks, months, and well into the following year, Moon Song took his adult students, warriors and hunters all, on long excursions into the hills, mountains, and river valleys. There he shared the hidden secrets of the most elusive animals. The weather did not matter, as each season revealed additional information.

When the hunter's quarry was observed in its natural habitat, Moon Song identified himself to the animal in question. Informing the hunters of each creature's name, Moon Song revealed how to take its life. He told his animal friends, through the power of his songs, that they would be hunted, but only in times of need. He swore no animal would ever lose its life without cause. He further promised each that their names would always be honored in song and that their children would never be hunted.

Thus it developed that, as Moon Song grew in years, his mystic voice became the guide of every hunter in the tribe. Before he would instruct them in the art of tracking and hunting any quarry, the apprentice hunter had to swear he would respect the animal and give its spirit proper dignity in life and in death.

By the time Moon Song reached adulthood, nearly every animal secret had been acquired by Ndee hunters. No one knew more about the animals than Moon Song, and no student ever completed training without understanding the value of each life taken. Fallen Oak was proud of his son, and his family relished the fact that their relative had become the spirit voice of all woodland creatures.

This was the way things remained for many years. During that time, Spirit Feather watched with careful scrutiny how each hunter was meticulously taught about which animals to hunt and which creatures were to be left alone. No hunter ever took it upon himself to question the reason for the special care, and most were satisfied with hunting only to feed their families.

This all changed when an arrogant warrior named Little Hand took it upon himself to go beyond what he had been taught by Moon Song. He was a mediocre hunter who complained incessantly about the inconvenience of having to hunt only when there was a need. His friends and family explained to him that this was the only way to ensure there would always be enough animals to hunt. It was common sense wasted on someone not interested in the needs of a few otherwise worthless animals.

Though Moon Song's methods made good sense to some of the other hunters of the tribe, Little Hand was not in sympathy. He was seen growing more and more impatient with the careful control of the quarry. He pointed out how easy it would be to obtain a few dozen extra skins. These, he said, would bring wealth to the hunters. Furthermore, he stated that the animals themselves were perfectly willing to be hunted as long as their spirits were remembered. What could be more inviting?

Word soon reached the attentive ear of Spirit Feather who was well aware of Little Hand's growing popularity. He counseled the restless youth and warned him to curb his arrogance, lest it lead to unfortunate consequences. But, failing to convince the impatient youth, the medicine man began to worry. Unable to sway the shaman to his plans to make the tribe wealthy, Little Hand took his ideas to the council.

Many of the men who had originally sat on the tribal council were now dead, including Moon Song's father, Fallen Oak. Only the medicine man remained alive and remembered the days before Moon Song's gift. The new members were friends or acquaintances of the ambitious Little Hand whom they saw as the next leader of the tribe. His aggressiveness had already brought some notoriety to the people. At the same time, he was aware of Moon Song's promise to the forest, woodland, and desert animals.

Moon Song did not trouble Little Hand. The ambitious youth knew of his gentle teacher's power and felt no threat from someone who spent more time in the mountains than in the village. The problem for Little Hand was how to get Moon Song to help him with his scheme to make himself and the tribe rich in furs and pelts.

Learning of Little Hand's plan to use Moon Song to destroy a well established order of honorable hunting, the medicine man broke with tradition and sought out Little Hand instead. Finding him with a gathering of his followers, Spirit Feather again warned Little Hand, as well as any who would be lured by his words, that the gift of Moon Song was sacred. He who would remove it from his people would suffer a terrifying fate.

"Beware the day the mystic voice ends," warned Spirit Feather ominously. "On that day, you shall be hunted by his spirit and all who knew his song. Take from us that which was bequeathed by the Giver of Life, and our people will shun your spirit from every house."

"I am not afraid of prophecy!" returned Little Hand. "But I am afraid of hunger and cold and poverty. Our families are strong, and now they need to become masters of their quarry. We should have many beaver skins hanging on our lodge poles. We should give our wives more buffalo and bear robes."

"Such wealth would destroy our oath to the Mountain Mystic," reminded Spirit Feather. "Your fathers waited for generations for this voice. It has granted us a time of plenty. Your families do not want for food or clothing. The air is alive with the song of peace and tranquility. The animals have become one with our people. We have an understanding which can last beyond the lives of your children."

"We need our children to remember us as true warriors and not blood brothers to a flock of birds!" laughed Little Hand. "I believe we do not need the voice of the forest spirit any longer. We have learned enough. Now we must begin teaching the animals fear!"

"Your voice will be the smallest of all who hear it!" promised Spirit Feather. "I have given you fair warning. What you do now will become our children's legacy."

"What I do now, old man, will bring fame and wealth to our people!" shouted Little Hand. In this he was encouraged by his followers. "I know of a way in which other tribes will seek us out for trade. My plan is simple, and when it is completed, will be remembered as the triumph of Little Hand."

What Little Hand was plotting was not something Spirit Feather could learn from tribal members. Knowledge of this sort required meditation. That night he sang to the spirits and asked for guidance. Yet, even as he sang before the tepee fire, Little Hand was already executing his plan.

Keenly aware of Moon Song's habits, Little Hand followed the Mountain Mystic from the desert camp up into the woodland mountains. There, as was his habit, the gentle warrior sang to his friends of the forest. Little Hand watched with quiet envy as the Mountain Mystic spoke with every animal which came within his view. There was no creature which was not recognized by Moon Song. He knew each one by its spirit name. This infuriated Little Hand even more.

As he continued to watch with simmering jealousy, Little Hand studied the only impediment to his leadership. He realized he would have to discover a weakness in the Mountain Mystic before taking advantage of him. From his concealment, he observed the loving affection Moon Song used to summon the animals. There was power in his soft voice, and Little Hand made a quiet promise that the mystic's voice would soon be his. Much could be gained by remaining silent, and moments later his patience was rewarded.

The soft melodic chanting of Moon Song was alluring and hypnotic. Its magical quality reassured all the animals. They came from every direction in the woods to lie close by him while Little Hand, concealed nearby, watched and listened intently. There was something compelling in Moon Song's voice. It was slight but nonetheless quite apparent to the sensitive ears of Little Hand.

For nearly an hour he studied the various songs of the Mountain Mystic. Though nearly imperceptible, Little Hand detected the subtle tone in each melody which summoned a specific creature. Each time Moon Song chanted, he was in fact, calling animals to honor them. It was remarkable, but so simple. By shifting inflection and adding specific notes, his voice attracted scores of birds, and even caused changes in the weather.

Quick to learn, Little Hand soon acquired a dozen chants and memorized them. Though there were a number of animals he coveted, he desired certain creatures more than others. In the second hour, Little Hand eventually heard the chant he had been waiting for, one to attract the buffalo.

Without realizing it, Moon Song taught Little Hand how to summon forth the creatures he longed for. Practicing in silence, Little Hand was soon confident he could do as well as his mentor. This was what he had desired from the beginning.

Though it had been difficult, Little Hand managed to leave the area without arousing the suspicion of Moon Song. Anxiously he hurried down the mountain, stumbling and falling several times. He did not mind the bumps and bruises which he collected getting back to the camp. This new knowledge was too important to bother with anything else.

Once in the village, Little Hand quickly sought out his growing band of followers and assembled them in a remote section of the camp. Assured of privacy, he informed them that he now possessed enough magical power to win over the objections offered by unconvinced members of the tribe. Anxious to join him, his followers agreed to accept him as their chief.

The plan was simple, vowed Little Hand. He would see to it that his followers and the tribe would become wealthy beyond their dreams. Soon they would be able to trade with any tribe, obtain any garment, and secure any weapon, object, or other prize. The future promised power and security in the accumulation of furs, pelts, and other ornaments presently gleaned in small quantities.

The first thing Little Hand had to accomplish was to remove the two people who might object to his methods. With instructions not to harm them, Little Hand ordered his men to kidnap both Moon Song and Spirit Feather.

While Moon Song and Spirit Feather were kept away from the tribe, Little Hand ensured the cooperation of the council by informing them that the rest of the tribe would accompany him to a section of the desert prairie. There he would prove his power and leadership before them.

The tribe gathered on a wide, flat promontory which overlooked the prairie. Little Hand informed everyone that soon they would profit from his leadership. Seeing their faces display skepticism, he carefully prepared to demonstrate his deceitfully acquired power. Simultaneously, a well armed group of hunters prepared their bows. He began to sing.

The first prize Little Hand attracted with his song was a small herd of antelope. No sooner had he begun the melody, then the herd appeared and all the animals were immediately shot. This display of power and marksmanship impressed the crowd. Many of the women rushed to claim their share, while concerned clan members raised objections that too many antelope had been taken. They pointed out such slaughter brought no honor to the hunt, the spirits, or the dead creatures.

Undisturbed by complaints, and urged on by those who wanted further demonstrations, Little Hand again summoned a group of creatures. This time a flock of geese appeared and were brought down with a barrage of arrows.

As with the previous demonstration, Little Hand was praised, and the spoils were quickly divided. Again, there were objections, but this time only a few. The display of unleashed power over the animals began to divide the tribe. Some insisted they, too, needed additional hides, pelts, and furs, while others warned of tribal greed and dishonor.

Taking note that younger family members were beginning to quarrel with their parents while siblings argued among themselves that they were being excluded, Little Hand believed more creatures should be killed. Everyone would eventually be satisfied, he promised. And so again he sang out. As more animals were called and slaughtered, the division within the tribe became more prominent. In their haste to secure a share, tribal members ripped the limp bodies of the creatures to pieces with sharp tools and greedy hands.

The glut of destruction continued for nearly an hour during which time hundreds and hundreds of animals died and were claimed without any control or compassion. As the riotous slaughter continued, Little Hand was elated by his success. Unmindful of the dozens of fights and angry disputes he had created, he endeavored to double his numbers. His immediate ambition was to become powerful enough to summon the most sacred of creatures to the festival of death.

The seemingly inexhaustible bounty of animals caused the unruly mob to become drunk with praise for the feats of Little Hand. His followers urged the crowd to choose him as the new leader of the tribe. Eventually the warriors were pressured into echoing his name.

The council, who up to now had been silent, considered the wealth which Little Hand was offering the people. Only two of the ten members approved of what Little Hand was doing. The majority wondered what Moon Song would say when he learned of the wanton misuse of his power. That question was in the minds of many when someone announced that Moon Song and Spirit Feather were at last free and seen ascending the hill.

Dismissing Moon Song as a threat, Little Hand reminded the people that as long as he was leader, they would never have to be satisfied with only enough. Now they would be known as the wealthiest people in the region. The entire animal kingdom was theirs for the harvesting. He would see to it that everyone shared in the plunder. His promise raised a din of jubilation, shouting, and approval.

Convinced that no creature was beyond his power, Little Hand sang an order that vast herds of buffalo come immediately. His chant coincided with the arrival of Spirit Feather and Moon Song. The two men were appalled by the mounds of dead animals he had amassed.

Standing astride a mound of trophies, Little Hand, with his hands on hips, proclaimed to the approaching Moon Song and Spirit Feather that he would be chief and that the people would never need any other leader. He would bring the world of the animals to serve him as master. He would command the skies to bring forth rain and lightning. Ultimately, he would even command the Great Spirit.

Moon Song held his composure for several minutes and then, with eyes flaring in the noon day sun, flew into a violent rage. His thundering voice exploded across the prairie and the sky darkened and rumbled. At first, the people thought it was Moon Song's anger which had been unleashed. However, they quickly realized it was the sound of a gigantic herd of buffalo charging directly towards them from several miles away.

While the panic stricken tribe began scrambling for safety away from the onrushing stampede, Moon Song took his knife from its sheath and glared in the direction of Little Hand. The pretentious temporary chief saw his followers evaporate as Moon Song sprang towards him. Little Hand quickly considered ways in which he could defend himself from the fury of the enraged warrior and still escape the buffalo stampede.

The thunder of the buffalo increased as Little Hand quickly seized an opportunity to preoccupy the attacking Moon Song while giving himself time to flee. Seizing a stranded child, Little Hand lifted it and ran straight for the approaching tide of buffalo.

Once within range of the advancing multitude of black hooves, and the endless rows of spiked heads, Little Hand threw the child directly in their path. Realizing he had seconds to escape, he sped away, disappearing in the proximity of the desert brush. Spirit Feather, the council, and the remnants of the horrified tribe were petrified at the impending fate which roared towards the helpless child.

Viewing the crying child directly in the path of the stampeding herd of buffalo, they held their breath and prayed. What the tribe observed next was beyond the scope of courage. They saw a single figure speeding into view as if propelled by a bolt of lightning. The answer to their desperate prayer was Moon Song hurling across the plain with astonishing speed. In the space of several heartbeats, they saw him scoop up the child, run twenty feet, and drop him into a shallow hole in the ground. To ensure the child's safety, they saw him seal the hole with his body. Seconds later, the gigantic wave of buffalo surged over him.

The billowing dust, smoke, and hundreds of thousands of thundering, trampling hoof beats drowned out the high pitched screaming of the tribal women. Later that day, with the last of the herd disappearing into the horizon and the dust settling quickly, the returning tribe began searching for bodies.

It was not long before someone cried out he had found the hole into which the little boy had been dropped to safety. Lifting the stiff, dusty, but otherwise unharmed child from his enclosure, the warrior held the boy in his arms until the frantic mother rushed in to claim her son. Smothering the boy in a tight, joyous embrace, the mother thanked and praised the courage of her son's benefactor.

Noting Moon Song's absence, Spirit Feather urged the people to find his body. By the end of the day, after having spent hours searching, everyone concluded, and sadly suggested to the medicine man, that the body of Moon Song had been trampled into powder.

Although the search was intensified and repeated the following day, the result was the same. Failing to locate the body of Moon Song, Spirit Feather admitted the mystic voice was gone. It was also learned, though few cared, that no one had discovered the body of Little Hand.

Despite the fact that no one had located Little Hand or his body, it was promised by the council that if anyone found him alive, he was to be banished for his crime of cowardice. Later that night, a solemn and reverential funeral pyre was burned in honor of the missing Moon Song and the several dozen tribal members who had lost their lives in the stampede. The praises and honors were many and Running Deer, Moon Song's mother, accepted all in her son's absence.

Days later, a curious group of people decided to see if there was anything left of the prizes offered them by the late Little Hand. Searching everywhere, they found nothing except the deep grooved imprints left by the massive herd. Some in the group were curious about what, in fact, had happened to Moon Song. Did he vanish with the buffalo storm?

A delegation of friends and relatives of Moon Song gathered outside the medicine lodge of Spirit Feather. With ample gifts for his sources, the group beseeched Spirit Feather to consult with the Giver of Life as to the fate of their champion. Spirit Feather, who had been preparing for the reception, was only too glad to seek the whereabouts of the spirit of Moon Song.

With a gathering of people in tow, Spirit Feather journeyed across the desert and up into the mountain where Moon Song had often been found in meditation. There, with several prayers and chants to the sky guardian, the people asked the Giver of Life to return to them the spirit of the Mountain Mystic.

Instantly, the gathering saw a rodent racing across an open field under the shadowed wings of a large bird of prey. They saw the field mouse seized by powerful talons. The mouse secured, the majestic winged creature flew up and onto the outstretched arm of an oak tree. There, he sat momentarily and stared down at the gathering.

The immense white bird's head bobbed and weaved from side to side as if trying to focus on the approaching group. Even with the acuity of its wide circular eyes, it appeared to be straining to identify the people. Asking the others to wait a distance from the tree, Spirit Feather slowly approached the snowy white bird. He was positive he had never seen its kind before. It was magnificent with its large inset eyes, so prominently featured in its feathery head.

The shimmering white bird continued to sit erect on the tree limb, allowing Spirit Feather to hear the shrill squealing of the field mouse it held in its claw. The rodent seemed to be in great agony. Spirit Feather observed closely how the head of the bird continued to bob up and down, and side to side, as if trying to focus his image.

The intuitive medicine man smiled broadly as he realized that the eyes of the white bird revealed who it was. Spirit Feather's heart soared to see that the Giver of Life had indeed returned the spirit of Moon Song to his people.

"Do you not recognize your old friend?" asked Spirit Feather of the shimmering white bird which continued to bob and weave its head as several other tribal members advanced. "Do you not know your mother? She is with us. We know it is you, Moon Song. Do you not know us?"

"Whoooo, Whoooo," was the only word offered by the strange bird.

"I am your brother, Moon Song. Don't you know me?"
"Whoooo, Whoooo," returned the bird once again.

Then it struck Spirit Feather why the bird could not speak. The prophecy had come true. The magical power of Moon Song had been taken away from the tribe. In its place the Giver of Life had returned the first owl. As for the spirit of Little Hand, the medicine man had only to hear the squealing field mouse to realize the answer.

Forever the Ndee would remember the courage and magical chants of Moon Song. Every time they encountered an owl in the forest, they would ask if he could recognize one of the Ndee as his own. The only reply ever given by the owl was to question the identity of the voice.

The Legend of the Forest Children

The Southwest is the home of many legends. Each one is a story in itself. Each evokes a memory of a time when an ancient people dwelled in the land we now call the western states. Many record the origins of a variety of tribes who inhabit the region. They are based on oral testimony of present-day people who cherish their ancestral spirits.

All the legends of the ancients have a common thread. They recall a time when a living spirit roamed the earth as a human being. These legends are part of an ingrained culture which seeks to preserve respect for the earth spirits by telling stories of the original inhabitant. Despite similarities, each story speaks of particular spiritual beings who lived, died, and left an indelible mark on the history of a proud nation. This is one such legend.

Long ago, in the year of the White Crow, a snowstorm struck the land. For several weeks the earth was blanketed by continuous snowfall. Few creatures ventured out into the white landscape. The people who lived here were called the Ndee, otherwise known as the children of the Giver of Life or Great Spirit.

It was hard for the Ndee that winter. In the desert where they lived food was scarce. The year of the White Crow would prove to be one of immense scarcity. It was difficult and cruel. Necessity evaporated the tribe's emergency supply of foods. In addition, the nearby woodlands, a main source of fresh food, had become a graveyard of skeleton trees whose bare arms mimicked the misery of the people. The hunters of the tribe spent much of their time seeking food. Some went in search of the migrating herds. Others searched the rivers and streams for fish, otter, and beaver. Some sought neighboring tribes to trade with. All were desperate.

The largest group of hunters was sent to look for food high up into the mountains. Theirs was a doubly difficult task. They not only had to track elusive game in the deep snows, but had to climb the mountain and challenge the mountain mists as well. This arduous task not only tested the mettle of the individual, but also the fabric of his determination.

There were twenty-five Ndee in one hunting party. Each had a reputation which spoke honorably of its owner. Yet none had a reputation more enviable than their leader. His name was Gray Wolf. His was the second voice in the great council and he was being groomed to be the new chief when his father, Two Bears, died.

Gray Wolf was his father's eldest son. His younger brother Red Wolf admired him greatly. At the age of eighteen, Gray Wolf earned his name in what many considered the greatest contest of courage ever beheld in the camp.

The incident occurred quite by accident. A pack of starving wolves raced through the Ndee camp in hot pursuit of an elk. They realized too late that they had blundered into a camp. Frightened, disoriented, and panicked, the wolves scattered in all directions.

The people of the camp were in the middle of a rehearsal for an upcoming ceremony when the wounded elk and the trailing wolves came crashing through. The wolves had no intentions of attacking people of the village, but when they realized where they were, the leader of the pack reacted defensively with growls and barks threatening anyone who might consider engaging them.

The tribe hesitated a second and then acted. The women and children screamed and ran away in fear; the men scrambled for their knives, clubs, and stones. Sudden panic by the frightened populous caused the wolves to attack but with little conviction. Their actions were self-protective.

The warriors of the tribe had no way of knowing the wolves only wanted to escape. They saw them as a danger to their families and responded accordingly. The warriors began throwing spears, clubs, and axes at the wolves. Many of the animals were wounded. Once blood was shed, the wolves attacked in earnest.

The accidental melee escalated as the savage animals attacked the Ndee. In their fury and desperation the wolves dove headlong into groups of people. Some were armed, some were not. The wolves flashed their teeth and leaped onto the warriors, biting and clawing. The warriors speared, slashed, and clubbed back.

Moments after it began, the wolves were struggling and fighting desperately to survive. Their enormous leader, a beast of great dimensions, claimed eight lives in rapid succession. He was set to attack a ninth when a Ndee warrior with a glinting knife in his hand sped across the crowded compound and took to the air with a great leap. With teeth clenched tightly he flew across the distance between him and the wolf before the wolf reached its intended victim.

The wolf pack leader was a full grown adult with many savage victories to its credit. The weight of the warrior crushed and sent him to the ground, yet few eyes were able to follow the speed he used to recover and turn on his assailant. With a precision born of raw power, the two tore at one another.

It was perhaps due to the skill taught to him as a young man that the warrior was able to grip the violently thrashing mane and hold the slashing teeth of the wolf to minimum destruction. In between the wolf's lightning bites and flesh-rending claws, spectators saw the warrior thrust a knife into the struggling beast. Both combatants were now drenched in blood. Finally the warrior prevailed. Exhausted, he lay still. In what seemed like hours but which was in fact only moments, the fight between the wolves and the people of the village was over. Once the pack of wolves saw their leader killed, the survivors scrambled recklessly out of the Indian camp with pitiful cries and wails of howling sorrow.

The honor of having killed the pack's leader went to the eldest son of Two Bears. As was Ndee custom and tradition, his name was changed to Gray Wolf. This was their way of honoring both the man and the slain animal. The spirit of the wolf would continue to live in the heart of the warrior. Because Gray Wolf's younger brother was among those who had helped subdue the pack, he shared in the credit. His name was changed to Red Wolf. His elder brother was proud of him and said so at the council fire. Red Wolf never knew he could stand so tall. His heart soared into the sky.

It was an honor for Red Wolf to stand proudly with his older brother. In the campaigns which followed he grew to admire him even more. Gray Wolf could see the regard in his brother's eyes. He too loved and praised his younger brother for displaying dexterity and speed as a warrior.

Throughout the camp, the people of the tribe honored them, believing they possessed "wolf power" *Mba biy.* They saw that there was no envy in either brother, that, on the contrary, they respected each other greatly. This also made the people proud.

It was these two brothers who now led the hunting party up into the mountains to seek supplies. With his older brother far ahead leading the group, Red Wolf reflected on their past glories. He wondered what great destiny life had in store for them. Yet these dreamy thoughts had to give way to the urgent needs of his task. The tribe was desperate for food and he, like the rest of the warriors, concentrated deeply.

While trudging through the deep snows he realized this was not a normal winter. Autumn did not glide easily over the land of the Ndee, he thought. It descended harshly like the foot of a vengeful giant. It came fast and furious, and, as if it were mocking the inhabitants, produced the most ghostly desolate landscape he'd ever seen. Everywhere the signs of death flirted like the wisps of an evasive ghost.

The biting winds stinging their exposed flesh, the group continued its search in the alpine wilderness. In their misery they often fell headlong into drifts and valleys. They scoured the many hills, cliffs, and upper peaks of each mountain. But in the end, they found only meager subsistence.

With great reluctance, the warriors in the mountains began the long trek back home. Their leader, Gray Wolf, suggested they break up into small teams and continue to search for food taking different routes home. The men agreed and quickly paired off. Red Wolf would accompany his older brother Gray Wolf. All promised to meet at a prearranged rendezvous point. The brothers began a trek into the snow-laden forest.

With their comrades off, Gray Wolf and his brother began walking down the mountain through the deep snow. Being from a desert tribe, they had little knowledge of the secrets of the upper mountains. They expanded their knowledge when they stepped on a large twig creating sharp noises which reverberated loudly and produced a most deadly avalanche.

After digging out of the avalanche, the brothers were more careful where they stepped. Their education continued with slips, falls, and half-a-dozen tumbles down the slippery slopes of the high mountain. Eventually they slipped once too often and rolled a long way down the sharp icy slopes quite unable to stop. With a painful thud they finally landed in a flat clearing at the bottom of the mountain.

Emerging from their snowy tomb, they came face to face with an old woman. Gray Wolf helped Red Wolf up, and both concentrated on the mysterious figure. She appeared to be floating on a bank of snow. With great difficulty, they approached the large drift on which she stood, but unlike the woman, the brothers sank into the snow to their knees when they attempted to climb up onto the bank.

"Who are you?" was Gray Wolf's question as he struggled in the snow. "Where do you come from?"

"I am Woman of the Forest," she explained, studying the two. "You may call me Wind Woman. This is my home. Why are you here?"

"I am Gray Wolf," replied the oldest, adjusting his footing on the soft snow. "This is my brother Red Wolf. We are the sons of Two Bears. Our home is at the bottom of this mountain. We are here with our companions seeking food for our people."

"You are foolish," Wind Woman said, glaring at the two as they continued to struggle in the soft white snow. "This is not the time of year to be hunting food. You should have prepared for the season."

"Our people did not think the snow would come so soon, or so hard!" declared Red Wolf. "But if we make it through this terrible winter, we will do better next time."

"Your people will not survive another season," corrected Wind Woman. "They will die in this one."

"I cannot believe that!" declared Gray Wolf. "So long as there is life, there is hope. As long as we live, we must not give up!"

"That remains to be seen," added Wind Woman with a cackle in her aged voice. "I do not suffer from the wants of hunger. You see, in my house there is always enough food."

"If that is so," stated Gray Wolf respectfully, "I am here to ask if we might trade for your goods."

While she spoke to his brother, Red Wolf studied the old woman. There was no doubt she resembled aged women of his tribe. Her skin was wrinkled and faded. Her body was thin and draped with loose fitting rags which fluttered in the breeze.

If there was anything mysterious about Wind Woman, it would be that she wore no heavy clothing against the biting winds or the intense cold. Red Wolf and his brother were protected with bear coats, yet she had but a light shawl. Red Wolf concluded she must be a spirit of great power.

"You have nothing to trade," replied Wind Woman. "However, I might be willing to play a game for my stores." She gave out a loud cackling laugh and it shivered the heart of Red Wolf. Gray Wolf was affected, too, but his concern was for his brother. Gray Wolf had concluded also that he was dealing with a formidable power. He knew about spirits.

"I will play this game in place of trade," agreed Gray Wolf. "But you must allow my brother to return to our village."

"But I want both of you to play," laughed Wind Woman. "Come, you will see my house and all it contains." She turned and moved away, with Gray Wolf and his brother following cautiously at a distance. Wind Woman led them across the clearing and deep into the dark snowy woods. The winds began to cry ominously.

The brothers exchanged wary glances; they had concluded they would be gaming with a spirit. The old woman arrived at a mysterious section of the forest and raised her voice in a magical chant. Instantly light illuminated a gigantic tree, and the winter storm abated. The brothers stared up at the tree's branches which seemed to reach high up into the wintry skies above them. Gray Wolf suspected twenty men with their arms extended could not have encircled the trunk of the tree.

The tree trunk protruded out of the snow. Its base was not unlike a great round lodge. Its rotund surface was rough and contained several doorways. Each door was duplicated on a dozen upper levels. Each level was a branch, and each branch had doors. The entire structure reached a height beyond his eyesight.

While the brothers stood awed by her tree, Wind Woman sang out again, and this time the doors on the lower levels opened to reveal well-lit tunnels or hallways. From their vantage point, the brothers observed that each hallway led to a great pile of stored goods. They could discern a great many baskets of corn, dried meat, fish, and an abundance of seeds and nuts. All in all, it was a great cache of food which could easily alleviate their own people's hunger.

His mouth was watering, but Red Wolf became aware of his brother's strong arm on his shoulder. Turning to see what his brother was looking at, he saw the old woman smiling again. In her eyes they detected a gleam. What kind of game could she have devised which would produce such a secretive grin? What was she after? It was apparent to Red Wolf that more than an ordinary game was at stake.

Gray Wolf, too, had been staring at the hoard of food. However, his inner resolve warned him that death was present. His guard was up; his spine twitched nervously, and he occasionally sent his eyes toward the outer circles of their position. He did not care for Wind Woman's enticing home. What price did she place on her stores? Something told him that this game involved death.

"Will you play for what your people need?" the old woman asked tauntingly. "Are you ready to game with me?"

"We will play this game if it is only a game," replied Gray Wolf suspiciously. "But you must assure us that if we play, the risk is worth the reward and not merely illusion."

"Yes," added Red Wolf. "How do we know that the food we see, is really there? And will you allow us to know the rules of your game before we start?"

"The food is real," smiled Wind Woman coyly, inviting them to the first hallway of her home. "It is as real as your senses. The reward will have all the reality of your courage and skill. Come, play this game with me and you will have the chance of feeding your families and becoming renowned within your tribe. This is life, the circle of death."

"If courage is to be the measuring rod by which we chance death," remarked Gray Wolf while approaching the first door to the great tree house, "then our reward will be easily obtained."

"Will you explain how the game is played," requested Red Wolf, following his brother to the first wide doorway.

"The game is simple, little ones," explained Wind Woman pointing into the long well-lit hallway. "All you have to do is to run into my house and take what you will. Once you have what you want, run back out and go home."

"And we keep what we take?" asked Red Wolf surprised by the ease of the contest. "All that we can take?"

"All that you can take," answered the old woman smiling.

"How much time are we permitted inside your home?" asked Gray Wolf. "How much time before you kill us?"

"That depends on your speed as runners," mused the old woman, eying the two cautious warriors. "I will allow you all the time you would give a thief whom you caught in your home. The tree is my home and it has served me well against intruders. But it is not without danger. If you run fast and quietly, you may be in and out before the tree even suspects you are taking anything at all."

"And if we awaken the defenses of your tree?" asked Red Wolf, realizing the fate in store for them.

"Why, in that case," finished the old woman with a satisfying leer, "you will become a fixture in my home forever!" The old woman laughed so loudly that her raucous noise made the two warriors shudder. It sounded threatening and insulting. The two returned hard looks at one another and then took positions near the doorway.

Seeing that the two warriors were prepared to game with her, the old woman stopped laughing and stepped away from them saying, "You will each have a door of your own." She led Red Wolf to another door which looked remarkably like the one his brother now stood at.

The two brothers gave one last look at each other and then prepared to game with the Wind Woman and her magic tree.

"Now!" shouted Wind Woman as she clapped her hands together. No sooner had she done so, then the two warriors were gone from her sight. She looked down the hallway that Gray Wolf had darted into and saw that his speed was incredible. In an instant he had sped away becoming nothing but a blur.

Gray Wolf realized that the tunnel was much longer than he had imagined. Still, with his speed he reached the stores of food and, wasting little time, gathered a large sackful, threw it on his back, and turned to retrace his steps. He was off. Although a bit unsteady, he still made good time. Then he noticed that the tunnel walls were shrinking.

Red Wolf had apparently made the same observation as he made his way out of the magic tree. The way out seemed longer than the way in. Yet determined as he was, he gathered all his resolve and shot towards the dimming hole which was the entrance door. No sooner had he cleared the threshold when a mighty slam behind him informed him he would have been crushed had he been slower.

Gray Wolf was pleased his brother had escaped the power of the tree. As he arose from the ground where he had landed upon exiting the tree, he smiled at his brother, who met him with an arm extended. The old woman was standing in one of the lit doorways calmly observing the two triumphant brothers.

"You each have but a sample of my stores," remarked Wind Woman, shrugging her thin shoulders. "What you took will be gone before too long. Won't you game with me again, and perhaps take more of what you need?"

"What we have, we are grateful for," answered Gray Wolf, lifting his heavy sack over his shoulder. "It was desperation which caused us to game with you. But we shall not soon forget your home or our narrow escape."

"The game you play is dangerous for those not prepared for the magic of your house," added Red Wolf, turning to follow his brother with his sack over his shoulder. "But it will be other little ones who will become fixtures in your tree."

"I will be here when you wish to game again," reminded Wind Woman, laughing as they turned to leave. "There is nothing so demanding as the gnawing of one's stomach. And since you are feeding a tribe, the demand will bring you back even sooner."

When Gray Wolf and his brother returned to their village with their bags of food, they became instant celebrities and were honored by the throngs which surrounded them. The food was quickly distributed to the hungry children and the old, and what was left was shared by the rest. Much happiness was produced, and soon the people, their hunger satisfied, gathered to hear the story which Red Wolf would repeat often.

Many of the other warriors wondered why the two brothers had not consented to challenge the old woman for more of her food. It was obvious that the amount they brought would soon be exhausted and winter was but half over. The brothers tried to explain that the forest guardian was not merely an old woman, but a witch, a spirit, a power, hungry to destroy those equal to her games.

Regardless of the warnings, a dozen warriors decided to return to where Red Wolf said the spirit lived. The chief was unable to persuade them to listen to the warnings of the brothers. There in the black woods, Wind Woman met the foolish warriors and challenged them all to game with her. With little hesitation or respect for the powers of the wood witch, the warriors chose doors. They were exactly as Red Wolf had described. One by one the warriors sped off and before long the contests were over.

When the warriors did not immediately return, the tribe hoped they were only slow, being burdened by the rich stores they had won and were bringing back with them. After twenty days, some began to wonder what could be causing the delay. More warriors ventured into the mountain forest and brought back the unhappy news that the men who had gamed with Wind Woman were never coming home. They had died in their attempts.

There were two reasons why Gray Wolf and his brother decided to return to the magic tree. The first was to try and negotiate the release of their comrades, and the second was that the stores of food which they had obtained had been exhausted. There were still three more months of winter left, and hunger was once again a noticeable visitor in the camp.

The old woman was pleased to see the Wolf brothers come back to game with her again. The talented and swift brothers did well in a dozen contests. They managed to return with enough food for the village to last out the winter. But, in their last contest to win the release of their comrades, they themselves did not return.

It was expected that Gray Wolf and his brother would need additional time in trying to recover their comrades from the forest witch. Finally, when spring arrived to relieve the misery of winter, the people of the village recovered from their weakness and grew strong again. They noted that the brothers' absence was marked by a strange new wind. It resembled the satisfying laughter of a triumphant old woman. The people became concerned.

The chief of the tribe led a hunting party up into the forests to seek the whereabouts of the missing brothers. There he saw that the renewed land was warm, clean, and fresh. New trees grew everywhere and the smell of pine was strong. When the group reached the spot there the tree house last stood, they found only ordinary tall trees in the area. There was no sign of the brothers.

The chief asked his guides if they were sure of the location. The guides assured him they now stood where the magic house had last been seen. Even after a concerted effort, no trace was found of the courageous brothers, the tree, or the witch. Surmising they had died at the hands of the mysterious witch, the chief abandoned the search and returned home.

The brothers were honored with a ceremonial funeral. In his prayers, the medicine man asked the Giver of Life that their lives and their memory become a part of the spirits of the forest. In honor of their sacrifice, their story became a song of the tribe's storyteller. Soon the children were chanting songs of praise for the speedy spirits of Gray Wolf and Red Wolf.

Not long after the funeral of the two brothers a strange occurrence took place. The children of the tribe were accompanying their mothers in the annual spring search for herbs, wild berries, and nuts. The women's search took them near the area where the magic tree once stood. Upon arriving, the mothers playfully asked the children to help look for the plants, nuts, and berries.

The children were inexperienced, and their mothers expected little from them. They assumed they would return with baskets full of odds and ends, but not much more. The children had hardly been gone a few minutes, when they returned from the woods with a dozen baskets full of delicious nuts, seeds, and berries.

When their surprised and delighted mothers asked where the children had discovered the food, the children eagerly and excitedly led them to an open area where a dozen varieties of seeds and nuts lay on the ground and wild berries grew everywhere on the nearby vines. The mothers tasted the fruit and nuts and found that they were the best they had ever eaten. The children, too, found them to be a great delicacy.

Curious that the children had discovered such a wondrous place, the mothers questioned the children about what had led them there. The children gleefully pointed up into the tall trees saying, "They did!"

The mothers looked up into the tall pine trees and saw two beautiful creatures scurrying across the long limbs and gliding freely from branch to branch. The animals were seen running inside the body of the tree and returning to drop seeds, nuts, acorns, and other delicacies to the ground.

With their baskets full, the women returned to the village and related what their children had discovered. Word of this reached the leader of the tribe. After listening to the amazing story and unable to explain the bounty the women had produced, the chief returned to the place with the elders of the village. To their amazement, everything the women reported was true.

Playing in the trees were an assortment of tiny black, gray, and brown creatures with bushy tails and sharp pointed teeth, gathering acorns, nuts, and berries. On closer scrutiny, the chief realized that the industrious little animals were gathering and storing food inside the trees of the forest.

The chief suspected that these animals were in fact the spirits of his warriors who had lost the game to the old woman of the forest. Two of the animals were nearly identical in color and design. Both possessed amazing abilities and displayed remarkable courage in their close proximity to the chief and the council of the tribe.

These animals, like other creatures of the forest, were treated with reverence and respect. They were accepted as the spirits of the lost warriors. Today, these speedy little creatures are called "children of the forest," or tree squirrels. Oddly enough, the fastest and most aggressive of the species are known as "wolf squirrels."